HELP!
My Dog has a
Canine Compulsive
Disorder

Toni Shelbourne

Other titles by the author

HELP! My Dog is Scared of Fireworks
Toni Shelbourne and Karen Bush
Help! My Dog Doesn't Travel Well in the Car
Toni Shelbourne & Karen Bush
Help! My Dog is Destroying the Garden
Toni Shelbourne & Karen Bush
The Truth about Wolves and Dogs
Toni Shelbourne (*Hubble & Hattie*)
Among the Wolves: Memoirs of a Wolf Handler
Toni Shelbourne (*Hubble & Hattie*)

Copyright © 2018 Toni Shelbourne and Karen Bush
Images copyright of:
Clouded Leopard TTouch, Ear Work (1), Tail Work (all) © Bob Atkins and David & Charles: Ear Work (2), Thundershirt © Sarah Fisher: Body wrap diagram © Karen Bush: Confidence course (2) © Sarah Fisher: TTouch Mouthwork A ©Bob Atkins and David & Charles: All other images © Toni Shelbourne.
Cover image: istock

The right of Toni Shelbourne to be identified as the author of this work has been asserted in accordance with the Copyright Designs and Patents Act 1988. All rights reserved. No part of this book may be reproduced or transmitted in any form without the prior written permission of the copyright holder.

Disclaimer
While the author has made every attempt to offer accurate and reliable information to the best of her knowledge and belief, it is presented without any guarantee. The author does not accept any responsibility in any manner whatsoever for any error or omission, or any loss, damage, injury, adverse outcome, or liability of any kind incurred as a result of the use of any of the information contained in this book, or reliance upon it. Please bear in mind that the advice in this book is not intended to replace veterinary attention.
If in any doubt about any aspect of welfare, care and treatment, readers are advised to seek professional advice.
ISBN: 1985232820
ISBN-13: 978-1985232822

This book is dedicated to all
Toni's dog clients
who have taught her so much
about helping others with
Canine Compulsive Disorder.

ACKNOWLEDGMENTS

I am hugely grateful to all those who offered suggestions, and so generously shared their time and knowledge. I have done my best to ensure that the information contained within is, as far as I can ascertain, correct at time of writing: if there are any errors, then the fault is entirely mine, and not that of those who so kindly put up with my many queries!

Among those I would like to thank are: Sarah Fisher, Robyn Hood, Rachel Windsor-Knott, Lisa Tenzin-Dolma, Rachel Hayball & David & Charles.

Toni wishes to give a big thank you to Karen Bush. Toni wrote this book but it would not have been possible to publish it without Karen doing the boring bits of formatting, covers etc.

For simplicity, throughout this book, dogs have been referred to as 'he'.

The acronym CCD used throughout this book refers to Canine Compulsive Disorder.

CONTENTS

3
Foreword
by Lisa Tenzin-Dolma

5
Introduction

7
PART ONE
What is canine compulsive disorder?

14
PART TWO
Possible causes of canine compulsive disorder

24
PART THREE
Observations

30
PART FOUR
Calming the environment, emotions and conflict that may trigger CCDs

37
PART FIVE
Equipment and tools to manage your CCD dog
Long lines – Stroking the leash - muzzle training - crate training

50
PART SIX
Mental stimulation and enrichment
Exercise – Enriching walks – Dog activities to enrich your dog's life – Garden activities – Summer day entertainment – Chews – Brain Training – Real Dog Yoga – Training

78
PART SEVEN
Finding methods to support your CCD dog & influence behavioural changes for the better
Tellington TTouch: *TTouches – Body wraps – Thundershirt – Confidence Course –* Other Holistic options: *Flower remedies – Homeopathy – Applied Zoopharmacognosy – Pet Remedy - Adaptil - Herbal Remedies and Nutritional Supplements –* Diet – Drugs

136
FURTHER READING

138
CONTACTS & RESOURCES

143
NOTES: Research Papers

145
ABOUT THE AUTHOR

FOREWORD
by
Lisa Tenzin-Dolma

*INTODogs Certified Canine Behaviourist,
founder and principal of The International School
for Canine Psychology & Behaviour (ISCP),
founder of the Dog Welfare Alliance,
co-chair of The Association of INTODogs,
and author.*

Canine Compulsive Disorder (CCD) is the term used for a condition that's very similar to Obsessive Compulsive Disorder in humans. It's distressing to see dogs displaying behaviours such as compulsive licking, sucking, tail-spinning, light chasing, pica and fly-snapping, to name but a few, and it can be physically damaging, as well as psychologically disturbing, for the dogs concerned. In this thoroughly researched and very valuable resource, Toni Shelbourne offers a wonderful selection of methods that you can use if you have a dog with CCD.

As there can be a number of causes, both physical and emotional, Toni explores these in depth. They emphasize the importance of close observation to pinpoint the triggers for these behaviours, so that you can take steps to pre-empt them and act swiftly before your dog becomes too entrenched to be receptive to distraction. The chapters include steps you can take, such as creating a calm environment, paying attention to diet, enriching the environment and engaging your dog's brain, and using modalities such as Tellington TTouch and other therapies.

Having adopted several dogs whose previously highly stressful lives precipitated CCD as a coping method, through working successfully to alleviate this, and through meeting many clients' dogs with similar issues, it appears that CCD has become a fairly common issue. Given that many dogs have experienced trauma in some form, and even more are expected to cope with spending long periods of time alone, this is hardly surprising. However, help is at hand in the form of this excellent book. So, please read on – the guidance offered in *Help! My Dog has a Canine Compulsive Disorder* will give you many pointers into how to make your dog's life (and yours) so much easier.

Lisa Tenzin-Dolma

INTRODUCTION

The term Obsessive Compulsive Disorder (OCD) is one I hear of in humans fairly frequently. People affected by this mental health condition experience frequent obsessive thoughts causing feelings of anxiety, disgust and unease, and act out certain behaviours over and over again. If left untreated, the condition can take over the sufferer's life.

There is some debate about whether dogs can obsess, as this would imply complex mental thought processes. This is why scientists mainly refer to repetitive behaviours in dogs as Canine Compulsive Disorder or CCD. Whether you believe dogs are capable of complex thought is by-the-by, but certainly they can show compulsive behaviours. You will see dogs repeating an action or behaviour out of context, such as continually chasing their tail, or constantly sucking an area of their body - to the extent even in some cases, of creating serious wounds. Others might eat inappropriate items like socks or stones, an act known as pica.

Whatever compulsive disorder your dog is showing, it is distressing for all concerned and best dealt with as soon as you realise a neurotic disposition is developing. You may have to turn detective to work out why your dog is demonstrating compulsive behaviours. There could be any number of reasons, (which will be explored further on in this book), but once understood, there are techniques you can use to help manage the condition and even helping to overcome it. Some individuals may have a lifelong tendency towards compulsive behaviours, but by recognising and dealing with the early onset of symptoms it is possible to deter a relapse in your dog.

Many of the management tools and all of the training methods described in this book can be applied to all repetitive behaviours. Some of the more common behaviours will of course be mentioned more frequently but I have tried to cover as many topics and points as I can. You can also contact me directly for advice if you feel you need specific help with your dog.

Toni Shelbourne

PART ONE

What is Canine Compulsive Disorder?

Canine Compulsive Disorder or CCD for short, is any behaviour or action out of context so it becomes abnormal. Dogs, additionally, will continually repeat the action and if not interrupted, it will often continue for a sustained amount of time. So, for example, tail spinning could be regarded as being rooted in predatory behaviour and a dog might chase his tail for hours at a time, becoming more and more frantic and aroused until exhausted and the tail sustains injuries.

This is different from phobic behaviour, where a dog may be frightened of an object, another animal, a human, or a situation and try to remove himself or force the trigger away. Once the trigger is removed the dog will calm down and doesn't display the phobic behaviour when out of the situation. So a dog scared of fireworks for example, will stop panting and digging once the fireworks stop and won't perform these behaviours at other random times.

CCD behaviours which are commonly seen include:

Light or shadow chasing: Chasing or pouncing on reflections from the sun on flooring, in water, or off man-made objects such as laser pens or watches.

Tail chasing: The repetitive action of the dog spinning around and catching his own tail. Some dogs will then worry or suck at it, or continue to spin on the spot whilst holding the tail in their mouth.

Flank or blanket sucking: The sucking of a dog's own body or an object like a toy or blanket. This could arguably be a follow-on from neonatal suckling behaviour but can start later in life or be related to a pain issue.

Licking objects: This could be bedding, floors, walls, windows etc. or even people, but is different from the dog licking himself.

Pica: The act of eating inappropriate objects such as socks and stones etc. Seen most commonly in gundog breeds.

Circling or pacing: Can be performed at different speeds and doesn't involve interaction with the tail. Can often be in just one direction but may be both ways.

Fly snapping: Sometimes called air snapping but basically seeming to snap at something in the air which doesn't exist. Dogs often do this behaviour with their heads raised.

Persistent barking: Dogs bark, some breeds more than others if they are bred to do so. They usually bark for a reason though, such as hearing a noise or for attention. CCD dogs may bark with no known trigger and it can be for a prolonged period of time. They may also appear to be in a trance-like state when they bark.

Toy or object fixation: When a dog is totally obsessed with something to the point of distress being caused if it is removed: or leaving the dog with it means he chews, licks, bites or stares at it

constantly.
Polydipsia and Polyphagia: Excessive drinking or eating. Of course, there could be an underlying medical condition for either of these, but for some dogs it is definitely a compulsion and is often a reaction to stress.
Hallucinations: Your dog may suddenly become anxious for no reason, staring at an area, refusing to come inside or just behaving really weirdly. It could be related to the fly snapping behaviour, or might be linked to another condition with a very similar name, Canine Cognitive Disorder, often referred to as 'doggy dementia'. However, this would generally be seen in older dogs and be accompanied with other symptoms such as disorientation, a shift in the wake/sleep cycle, and house training breaking down.

There are many reasons why your dog could be compulsive and it is a case of trying to work out why it is occurring. I will discuss some possible or most likely causes in the next chapter: not all are rooted in a medical problem. There is research to suggest that true Canine Compulsive Disorder, where there are anomalies in the brain, does exist so if you try all the methods and tools in this book and are still seeing a problem, it may help your veterinarian to pinpoint the condition and offer suitable medication.

Some research has been conducted on dogs to try to determine a cause of CCD and there are several theories. There is some evidence to suggest that abnormalities in the brain similar to humans with Obsessive Compulsive Disorder (OCD) could be the cause of flank sucking behaviour in Dobermann Pinschers. It appeared to not come from one area of the brain specifically and didn't mirror the human models in some areas, but one part of the brain to do with remembering and performing known tasks was indicated, hence the repetitive nature of the disorder.

Furthermore, whilst mapping DNA codes in dogs, the Broad Institute of MIT and Harvard have discovered a neural gene linked to obsessive compulsive disorder in flank-sucking Dobermanns, and identified the genes which lead to the various manifestations of CCDs in other breeds. If you would like to read these yourself, I have listed the studies in the Resource and Contact section. To be honest though, this disorder has had little research to date, but some exciting studies are being carried out as I write.

Another study conducted on tail chasing in Bull Terriers also produced an interesting hypothesis. Right at the end of the study in the discussion section, although they concluded that the probable cause was CCD or partial seizure disorder, they suggested that it also showed similarities to human autism. This was based on the dogs often being asocial, withdrawn, preoccupied with objects and could have a tendency towards explosive aggressive incidents and trance-like states.

Other supposed compulsive disorders might also be linked to partial or what is termed as focal seizures. For example, a seizure in the lateral hypothalamus, the area associated with predatory behaviour, could manifest in fly snapping. There have even been cases of inappropriate eating linked to seizures, although there were other symptoms related to this, resembling long bouts of staring, and making swallowing and gulping motions when not eating or drinking.

There may very well be a genetic component to the condition as there seems to be a strong case for it being an inherited disorder. For example, with flank sucking in Dobermanns and tail spinning in Bull Terriers, puppies from affected parents or grandparents often have a higher likelihood to go on to develop CCD themselves. Because of this potential it is worth asking questions of the breeder if you are looking at a puppy whose breed is associated with compulsive tendencies.

There is also often a suggestion in research papers that male dogs tend to be more susceptible to this. However, I have seen dogs of both genders with the condition. The age of onset seems most commonly to be between six to twelve months of age, but has been noted in dogs both younger and older than this.

There are certain breeds that appear to be predisposed to certain CCD behaviours, such as Bull Terriers and German Shepherds tail chasing and Cavalier King Charles Spaniels fly snapping, but any breed can be affected, so the list below is not exhaustive:

Flank Sucking and Lick Granulomas: Dobermann Pinscher, Great Dane, German Shepherd, Labrador.
Fly snapping: Cavalier King Charles Spaniel, German Shepherd, English Springer Spaniel, Dobermann Pinscher, Bernese Mountain Dog, Labrador, Airedale Terrier, Miniature Poodle, German Short haired Pointer, Border Collie, Irish Setter, and the English Setter.
Hallucinations: Dalmatian, German Shepherd.
Pica: Retriever breeds.
Shadow Chasing: Collie, Old English Sheepdog, Wire haired Fox Terrier, Rottweiler, Schnauzer, Golden Retriever, German Vizsla.
Tail Chasing: German Shepherd, Bull Terrier.

Compulsive acts appear to be linked to instinctual breed behaviours/jobs. Retriever types, who are heavily reinforced both genetically and by handlers to pick up and carry objects, can develop pica, and Collies can convert their predatory chase behaviour into shadow chasing instead of herding. Of course, where boredom or stress is a factor in the behaviour rather than an underlying medical or genetic reason, then ensuring an outlet for innate, hard-wired behaviours, or at least providing adequate mental stimulation may prevent compulsive behaviours from developing.

I have been unable to find any official statistics as to how prevalent it is, or which behaviours are most common, but an informal poll with dog training colleagues shows that the most frequently seen compulsive behaviours are persistent barking, shadow chasing and tail spinning, followed by fly catching, licking, chewing, spinning, pacing, flank sucking, toy obsession and pica. The least commonly seen were digging, and polydipsia with hallucinations and polyphagia not seen at all by any of the 108 people who took part in the poll. This may be too small a representation to show a true result but reflects my own experience with CCD cases.

Whatever the cause, if you notice your dog exhibiting any tendencies towards a compulsive behaviour, it is best for both of you if it can be dealt with as soon as possible, before the behaviour becomes ingrained and harder to change or your dog sustains serious injuries. If left unchecked it could severely affect you and your dog's lifestyle and interfere with normal activities such as going out for a walk on sunny days or leaving him unattended due to the damage he is causing himself physically.

The first action which you, as an owner, can take is to figure out the likeliest cause and discuss any suspected underlying health issues with your vet. It is paramount, for example, that you rule out pain as the root cause or any of the other health issues associated with the condition. Some CCD type symptoms will reduce or disappear completely once a health condition is treated. For other sufferers who have a clean physical bill of health, you can work with a qualified behaviourist or Tellington TTouch Practitioner to put an effective plan in place to manage, and re-train your dog to achieve a happier, more restful life.

PART TWO

Possible Causes of Canine Compulsive Disorder

Canine Compulsive Disorder, or symptoms that look like it, can be rooted in physical, psychological or neurological problems. The first port of call for any dog showing CCD-like symptoms is to visit your veterinarian. It is vital that you work out if the behaviour is coming from ill health or a psychosomatic origin so you can work out the best course of action. Take as much information as you possibly can to the consultation to aid in the diagnosis; reading Part Three on observations will help you to prepare. You can also video your dog in action for your vet to review.

Health
Many of the CCD-type symptoms can be rooted in a health problem, especially if all the other known causes are unlikely and the behaviour starts suddenly with no other changes to your dog's lifestyle, environment or external factors that could cause stress. Let's look at some of the most likely health reasons of your dog's behaviour:

Focal, (Localised) or Psychomotor seizures
Mentioned in chapter one, seizures and epilepsy often start around the age of six months to two

years and can look like a CCD. The common conception is that epilepsy involves convulsions but this is not always the case, and sometimes may involve an altered state of consciousness rather than loss of it. If your vet suspects seizures he will prescribe anti-epileptic drugs. Often the diagnosis comes from ruling out other causes so it can take some time and effort to reach this conclusion. Seizures occur when there is an abnormal electrical disturbance in the brain. In focal seizures, this can be limited to just one area and affect a specific part of the body. If it causes a psychomotor seizure, this involves a strange behaviour that could last only a few minutes such as tail chasing, air snapping, sudden and irrational fears, or staring into space. Sound familiar? Could a seizure be the cause of your dog's CCD symptoms?

Hypothyroidism

One of the early signs of hypothyroidism can be the onset of CCDs such as tail chasing and excessive grooming. Your dog may also be hyperactive, slow to learn, have increased anxieties such as separation anxiety, noise phobia, fear of people or other dogs, and suffer from aggressive outbursts to both people and dogs. These changes happen long before the physical issues appear, so if at around two years of age or later, your dog's behaviour starts to alter it is always worth ruling out thyroid problems.

The thyroid is responsible for producing a number of hormones which regulate the function of your dog's metabolism. Hypothyroidism (*hypo* meaning low) happens when the gland stops producing enough of these hormones either because of damage, or disease such as an autoimmune problem, where your dog's body starts to attack itself. A blood test to check the levels of liothyronine (known as T3) and levothyroxine (known as T4) can be taken but can give false readings, and a wider spectrum blood screening and other tests may be needed. Look up the work of Dr Jean Dodds, a world-renowned expert in canine hypothyroidism; for more information on full screening visit her website at

http://www.hemopet.org/hemolife-diagnostics/veterinary-thyroid-testing.html

If your vet is unable to offer you the tests you need, ask for serum to be sent to Hemopet in the States. It's not that expensive and will give you the gold standard in hypothyroid diagnosis.

Food intolerances and gut imbalances

Strange as it may seem, many dogs who obsessively lick carpets, windows, clothing, owner's arms or legs or their own lips, (but not themselves) could have dietary or gastrointestinal problems. The behaviour even has its own name 'Excessive Licking of Surfaces' or ELS. A study done at the University of Montréal Veterinary Teaching Hospital concluded that 74% of dogs with ELS had gastrointestinal disorders, (GI for short). These included eosinophilic and/or lymphoplasmacytic infiltration of the GI tract, delayed gastric emptying, irritable bowel syndrome, chronic pancreatitis, gastric foreign body and Giardiasis. When treatment was given 59% of dogs had significant improvements, with 53% being totally resolved.

Talk to your vet about diagnoses and treatment. If you suspect your dog has a GI disorder which is food related, ask your vet to refer you to a canine nutritional expert. Many holistic vets specialise in nutrition and other professionals exist who can help you and your dog. Look up the Facebook group Holistic Dog Care (a link can be found in the Contacts and Resources section) for further information, or if you suspect a diet-related issue, have your dog's possible intolerances tested: visit **www.nutriscan.org** for more information.

Cushing's disease, kidney failure and Diabetes Mellitus

All these conditions cause excessive drinking so need to be ruled out if your dog is suffering from polydipsia (excessive drinking).

Pain

Pain can go undiagnosed in dogs for a long time. This may be due to their predisposition for hiding discomfort but whatever the reason it can display in CCD-type symptoms. There are numerous ways in which dogs are able to tell us they are in pain. Some may worry at an area, licking or nibbling; others become hyperactive or agitated, and might pace or circle; or he might become reclusive and show reluctance to be touched.

Whatever way it manifests, it is worth ruling it out if you think it might be the cause of the behaviour. I have known tail spinners to have a problem in their backs, and excessive lickers to have arthritis, decaying teeth, digestive system pain or cancer; the list is endless. Older or injured dogs might not be able to reach the actual area of concern due to diminishing flexibility so the pain might not be the place he is worrying at, which of course makes it harder for your vet to pinpoint.

Work through the following checklist before seeing your vet, as the information may help with the diagnosis:

- Note any anomalies or changes in his general health, including changes in eating habits, stools, sleep pattern, areas of the body that

might feel bloated, discharges from any orifice etc.
- Take note of exercise tolerance, any stiffness after exercise or rest.
- Note any areas he seems reluctant to let you touch.
- Observe any hair changes such as swirls in the coat, quality or colour changes; there might also be scurf present in one particular area.
- Look at how he bears weight on his legs - is it even or does he stand with more weight on one side; or have one leg with much less weight; or maybe he leaves it out to the side or behind him.
- Check to see if any areas of his body feel tight in the muscle; or when you touch an area do you see any spasms in the skin?
- Does he appear hunched or tucked up in the belly area?

Make a note of *everything* you notice, no matter how trivial it might seem, as this will help your vet find the area of concern. You can also video your dog prior to the appointment, as under examination, many dogs have an adrenaline burst and this can cover up the problem. If you are unsure about how to spot gait anomalies or unusual posture patterns in your dog, find the nearest Tellington TTouch Practitioner or canine physiotherapist to help you analyse your dog's movement if you think it might be skeletal or muscular in origin. You could also talk to your vet about putting your dog on a pain trial, although depending on the source of the pain you may or may not see any changes.

If you have a hunch that his behavioural issue is

rooted in a pain issue, be persistent and ask for further tests such as ultrasound, x-rays and blood screening or get a referral to a canine osteopath or physiotherapist. Try to remember when the behaviour started and if it might be linked to an injury or trauma: maybe he got knocked over in the park by another dog and at the time seemed fine or was sore for a few days but then seemed to recover. Rack your brains, but do not dismiss pain as the root cause.

Head injury or tumours

The brain is a complex organ and we are only just now starting to understand the canine brain. It stands to reason that if a head trauma occurs it could affect function, and depending on which area of the brain is affected, could result in CCD-like symptoms. Likewise, a tumour can result in many behavioural changes.

Sensory function problems

If a dog's sight, hearing, sense of smell or touch is affected by injury, age or disease, this could result in an increased risk of a CCD developing.

Degenerative conditions

Canine Cognitive Dysfunction is what might be termed as dementia in dogs. It is known that most cases of compulsive disorders start in younger dogs so if your veteran starts acting strangely, cognitive dysfunction may be the problem. There are some good treatments on the market now for older dogs so discuss these with your vet.

Infection

A virus in the central nervous system might also present as abnormal behaviour.

Oxygen deprivation at birth

I have worked with one dog who was known to have been deprived of oxygen, and he had a number of CCD-type symptoms and behaviours. You wouldn't necessarily know if this had happened to your dog if he is a rescue, but life is never going to be easy for that individual or for the people who care for them. Asphyxia can cause later problems not only in the brain but the rest of the body too. Symptoms can range from autistic tendencies, to issues with vision, movement problems and seizures to name but a few.

If you have ruled out health problems, then it is necessary to eliminate other factors that could be contributing to the behaviour:

The human influence
Some dogs develop CCD because of inappropriate actions by us: for example, unfortunately, many people find it funny to let their dog chase the light from a laser pen or the reflections off a watch. This can set up a pattern of chasing any reflection for a bored or stressed dog. Or you might have laughed at him pouncing on the light coming in from the window. The dog, getting a reaction from you, may start to repeat the pouncing.

Ill-conceived actions can set up a lifetime of stress for both dog and guardian, with guardians inadvertently reinforcing the behaviour by then reprimanding the dog every time the act of light chasing occurs. Confusion sets in for your canine companion as he can't understand why this action is no longer wanted and praised - but by now the action is a habit.

For other dogs, any interaction with a human, even if it is a negative one, is better than none at all; dogs learn to display these behaviours so they get attention.

To determine if it is truly a CCD problem or a behaviour triggered by humans, see if the behaviour stops when you leave the room. It could be a reaction to one family member so others can tell you if the dog performs the behaviour whilst out of your (or others) presence or not. Alternatively, set up a camera to record your dog when he is alone. If the behaviour doesn't occur when you are not there, then question what you have done, or are doing, to trigger the CCD type behaviour.

Unknown causes
True Canine Compulsive Disorder may exist, along with other little-known conditions. Think back to the studies mentioned in Part One: so little is currently known, but in time new research should give us a greater understanding.

Autism could be one of those possible unknown causes. Let's remind ourselves of the research paper that hypothesised that some Bull Terriers with CCD tendencies may be showing signs of autism. Although not a definitive study, the researchers also indicated this condition in dogs could be linked to a genetic disorder called fragile X syndrome. Until more research is done we can't say for sure that dogs can be autistic, but we can say that they show autistic-like tendencies. As one of the key criteria to diagnosing autism in humans is repetitive patterns of behaviour, this characteristic could also be the root of the CCD in your dog.

If your dog is also showing some or all of the following indicators, you might suspect autism:
- Impaired social interactions.
- Unresponsive to you.
- Doesn't like to be touched.
- Seems shut down or uncaring of the world around him.
- Has difficulty learning or retaining commands.

- Can be aggressive.
- Needs a rigorous set routine.
- Gets obsessed with objects.
- Is very choosy about what he eats.

If we know so little about the condition in humans, we cannot begin to understand if dogs suffer from this too. A number of institutions in the States are collaborating on a study into canine autism and the results are bound to be fascinating. In the meantime, if autism is suspected, manage the triggers and keep your dog calm. Some of the Tellington TTouch methods described later in this book may help, especially the body wrap which is so useful for humans living with the condition. In fact, I would suggest all or most of the management tools in this book would be worth trying to improve your dog's life.

Stress/boredom/conflict

If all of the above causes can be ruled out then we must look at stress, boredom or conflict as the primary cause.

For many dogs in this modern age, life is difficult. They are often under stimulated, (especially intelligent dogs and working breeds), restricted in exercise and social interactions, and have everything in their lives controlled by us; when they eat, play, sleep, reproduce, don't reproduce etc. They may also be forced to live in a busy multi-animal household and not get on or feel safe around others of their own kind or even with us.

We need to first reduce any conflict and stress, and increase exercise and mental stimulation in order to start addressing canine compulsive disorder type symptoms. In the following chapters I will discuss ways to manage your dog and the environment around him and give you other tools in helping to change his behaviour for the better. But first we need to define the problem so you can tailor any changes you make to your dog's individual needs. In the next chapter I'll look at how to do this.

PART THREE

Observations

In order to determine why your dog is displaying a certain action, you first need to find the root cause. From the previous chapter some of you, if you have found a physical problem, may already have seen a reduction in your dog's CCD symptoms. For others, if the cause is stress, boredom, conflict or inappropriate interaction with you, then you may just be getting started on the section of the book that will help you. Observation in all areas of your dog's life is necessary to determine the required changes you may need to make for your dog to be more settled and content.

I suggest that first of all, you write down everything that happens to your dog on a daily and weekly basis, and answer the questions below. You may want to do this as a family if you live in a household with more than just you and your dog. It is interesting to note how your dog behaves differently with different people and also other people's observations of his issues/stresses etc.

Consider all the following questions:
- What CCD is he displaying?
- When does this happen? - Time of day/triggers/pattern/influenced by you/when is it worse?

- What happens just before he starts to perform these actions?
- How long does he perform these actions?
- Can the behaviour be interrupted and your dog diverted on to another activity?
- When did the behaviour start? At what age, were there any changes or stresses in yours or your dog's life at the time?
- Has your dog got or had any injuries or illnesses? (Refer to the last chapter)
- Can you safely touch your dog when he is in the middle of repeating this action?
- Does your dog have any other behavioural issues that need addressing?
- How much exercise does he get?
- Is the behaviour better or worse on days he gets less exercise?
- How much time does he spend alone when you are out of the house?
- Does he spend time alone when you are home? Is he isolated in a different part of the house away from company? (Include overnight if he sleeps in a different room from you).
- Does he have access to stimulating toys? And do you rotate them regularly to keep interest up?
- Do you do any training with him in which he has to use his brain or other senses than the one he is using in the compulsive disorder?
- Does he have access to a good and calm outside space or does he get stressed because of dogs next door or children banging on the fence etc?
- When does he get fed?
- Does he get any chews or treats during the day?

- How does he interact with all the humans in the house? Are there any people he is scared of or over aroused by?
- What is his breed's job? And does he get an outlet for that instinctual function?
- What stresses him out? Is it noises, people, objects, other dogs, other animals?
- How much sleep does he get and where does he sleep?
- Can he switch off or is he constantly on the go?
- What makes the behaviour decrease?
- Does the CCD occur every day? If not, what is different about the days he doesn't perform these actions?

Now you have a clearer idea, that everyone involved with your dog agrees on and has contributed to, let's go through the questions so I can explain their relevance:

Defining the problem

You can't manage or change a behaviour unless you know what it is, what happens just before it starts, when or why it happens and what makes it worse. Also, does your dog show more than one CCD or behaviour that needs addressing? Often we don't realise the depth of the problem or recognise a behaviour as being an issue if it is overshadowed by a larger, more challenging one. But one may be feeding the other, so it is good to know the base line, and it also means you can accurately note the changes as they happen. Sometimes it is easier to change smaller issues first, because these will be influencing the larger ones: and if tackling the main problem seems a bit daunting, then starting with simple changes that can be achieved quickly may help to motivate you to tackle the bigger issue.

Exercise

Lack of exercise is a huge problem for some dogs. Although dogs will, to a certain extent, adjust to the level of physical exercise you give them, it is not true for all. Age and breed are factors that may affect the amount of exercise your dog needs. Some are naturally more energetic than others and physical exercise will need to be increased or, if that isn't possible on some days, then he needs to be tired mentally instead.

Diet

As seen in the previous chapter, diet can be a contributing factor to CCDs. A healthy species-specific diet is essential for all lifeforms, including your dog. His food should not be about how cheap it is or how convenient it is for you, but about what he needs for optimum health. Over the past few decades a huge rise has been seen in health and behavioural issues in dogs and this can, in part, be put down to commercial low-nutrition kibbles.

Look at the ingredients list on the packaging of your dog's food. How many artificial preservatives and colours does it contain; what is the real meat content; does it contain mostly cereals and other fillers? Although better products will cost more because they have more expensive high quality ingredients, price does not guarantee a good product, so do research what goes in your dog's bowl. I am an advocate of high quality food, whether that is raw, home cooked or a good quality commercial product. I understand that it needs to be suitable for your dog and for you as an owner, but information is power, so do at least read up on the pros and cons of both kibble and raw/home cooked food before you make a choice. If you want to out find more, read some canine nutrition books, or consult a canine dietary consultant – you'll find information on these in the Further Reading and Contacts and Resources section. Diet can have a major impact on health and behaviour and many owners report an improvement in their dog's behaviour just with a simple change in the food they feed. It may not be the magic cure but might, long term, be part of the solution.

Boredom

Boredom is another huge factor for many dogs suffering from CCD. Dogs are social creatures just like us, and if alone a lot of the time, under exercised and given little mental stimulation, they can turn self-employed and come up with their own amusements. A physically and mentally satisfied dog is a happy one and I will discuss ways in which you can achieve those goals later on in the book.

Along with his dinner, having appropriate things to chew is essential for a dog's mental health. As well as keeping his teeth clean it will promote the release of neurotransmitters such as serotonin which is vital for a happy, calm dog. The chewing will also alleviate boredom and hopefully help divert him from his less suitable activities. I will discuss safe and suitable chews and boredom-busting toys in the following chapters.

The other boredom-relieving workout you can do, besides more physical exercise, is finding a breed-specific activity. Not all collies can herd sheep but you can teach him Treibball or agility; or go to a trick training workshop to learn some fun ways for you to wear him out. There are many methods to mentally stimulate your dog in the right way; with a little imagination it doesn't have to be expensive or time consuming – for example, twenty minutes of scent work can completely exhaust a dog and is easy to achieve at home.

Sleep time
Having said that, you do need to make sure your dog gets sufficient sleep. Like us, sleep deprivation can have catastrophic consequences for our canine companions. You know yourself what it is like if you have a lack of restorative rest. Make sure your dog's bed is positioned in an area where he can, whenever he needs, take himself off to snooze. For families with young active children, this is especially needed. If he doesn't naturally settle and is displaying signs of hyperactivity, then you will need to help him to relax and rest; more information on that later on in the book.

One of the biggest factors for your CCD dog, though, is to eliminate as much stress as you can from his life. This, along with managing his condition, together with all the points above, will be vital for change. You can already make some changes following on from what has been discussed in this chapter and the observations you have made: the next chapter will cover further practical changes to help him.

PART FOUR

Calming the environment, emotions and conflict that may trigger CCDs

By now you should have a clean bill of health for your dog from your vet and a list of potential triggers for your dog's CCD. These may fall into one or more of the following categories:

Environment: Things that happen around your dog in the home, on walks etc., that aren't related to humans or other animals, such as water reflecting off ponds which might be a trigger for his light chasing.

Emotional: He may have fears and anxieties or he might just be a very sensitive dog. You will find more help with supporting your dog emotionally in Parts Six and Seven.

Conflict: Does your dog get on with everyone in the house, including humans and other animals of all species? Is there a dog next door that winds your dog up through the fence and the frustration sets him off tail chasing?

Mental: Boredom, such as a working dog not doing the job he was bred to do; I will deal with this in detail in Part Six.

In this chapter let's take a look at how making some simple changes to your dog's environment, and addressing conflicts can help in managing potential triggers for some of the CCDs listed in Part One.

Light chasers
Reflection-proof your house and garden as much as you can - it might not need to be forever, but in the short term may help avoid your dog becoming upset while you are getting to the root of the problem and putting in the training and other suggestions mentioned elsewhere in the book.

If on sunny days your dog pounces on shadows coming through the window and you are unable to shut your dog out of that room, think about installing black out blinds or curtains sufficiently thick to stop the light coming through to prevent the chasing. If moving shadows are caused by plants outside the window, trim back any vegetation. It may also be beneficial to temporarily fit some opaque film on your windows to soften the light coming in. This is fairly inexpensive and easy to fit.

If none of these suggestions are feasible, how about buying some card or black paper and cutting it to the size of your windows so that on really sunny days you can block the light out quickly and efficiently by taping the card to the window or using Blu Tack. If you don't have curtains or a rail, maybe invest in a tension rail and just put up the curtain on the sunny days when you need to help your dog settle. There are many ways to block out light, you just need to be creative!

You can also swop water and food bowls for ones made of non-reflective materials, or move their location to somewhere else in the house away from sunlight.

Ban family members from wearing watches on

sunny days, and never allow anyone to tease your dog with reflections from anything shiny, including laser pens. It may seem funny to you at the time, but obsessive shadow chasing behaviour has been triggered in many dogs by inappropriate play with these types of items.

Experiment with artificial lighting to ensure no shadows are cast, even when people walk across the room. You may have to darken the room or invest in uplighters that don't cast a strong shadow on the floor.

Cover shiny laminate floors with rugs if the sparkle off it causes a problem for your dog, or roll out some dark rubber matting to diffuse the light when needed. This would also stop him damaging the floor, rugs or carpets and may be more forgiving on his paws.

Out in the garden, move any pots that reflect light on sunny days, and remove garden furniture that might cast a moving shadow, such as parasols that sway in the breeze. Screen off ponds where the light reflects off the water so your dog can't see it; even filling in gaps between fence panels where light seeps through is worth trying.

You could also change your walking routine on sunny days if the light chasing happens outside of the house. Channelling your dog's energy with mental games at home or walking him on a long line to avoid him running into ponds and spending hours barking and pouncing on the reflections in the water might be safer for everyone.

Tail chasing, fly catching, circling and pacing
What in the environment triggers these behaviours? Keep a diary for a few days and see if there is a pattern. Is it noise from your teenager's

music device or the weird sounds coming from their game on the Xbox or Play Station? If you and your partner argue, does this trigger it? Is it people arriving or leaving the house, the excitement of you reaching for the leash to go for a walk, the stress of going into a certain room or environment? Once you know the trigger, whether it is environmental, or emotional, then you can start to change it. This might be simple actions such as turning the sound down on the TV, or desensitizing cues like putting shoes on half an hour before leaving the house, or picking up and putting down keys often so that the trigger becomes the norm and doesn't pre-empt you leaving. Think about the trigger and then you can find a way to change your dog's response to it.

Persistent barking, digging, and scratching
As odd as it may seem if your dog is doing any of these, you first need to rule out the possibility that he can actually hear, smell or see something you can't. Turn detective and think outside of the box. Double check that you don't have insects or rodents under the floor boards, pipes that make a funny noise at certain times of the day, electric motors that whirl at a pitch that only your dog can detect. Dogs can hear in a range approximately twice as wide as humans and in the upper range the sound can cause physical discomfort. Check whether neighbours are using sonic equipment as a cat or fox deterrent, or if the fridge is vibrating, etc; try turning electrical equipment off instead of leaving it on standby, or put the fridge on blocks to see if it makes a difference.

It could be a smell that only he can detect. Dogs can be trained to detect blood in a large body of water, so it's not unfeasible that he is smelling something you can't; is there a long dead rat under the floor boards? Or is he scratching at the rug because it feels good under his feet and satisfies his need to dig - or does he do it in the same place if you remove the rug? Try changing the environment just a little to see if it influences a change in your dog's behaviour.

Toy or object obsession, chewing

I suppose the obvious answer is to remove the type of toy or the object they are obsessing on, but this may cause undue distress. If it is a certain type of toy, such as a soft toy, and if your dog is a bitch, make sure that she doesn't have a hormonal imbalance or is suffering from the trauma of losing puppies which can cause her to be grieving. A Zoopharmacognosy practitioner can help her with the grieving process if you suspect this might be the case (see Part Seven for more information on this modality). Some dogs want to hold on to toys or objects or chew as an emotional comforter, a bit like the comfort blanket which some children need. Chewing is a natural way of releasing stress for dogs, with the act of chewing producing feel-good endorphins in the brain, and can be very soothing. Check that your dog isn't obsessively chewing through stress, or in fact boredom. You might also want to get his teeth checked to make sure there are no problems in the mouth such as retained teeth. Sometimes excessive chewers can be out in the occiput - the bone that creates the bump on top of his head – and seeing a canine qualified osteopath or McTimoney Chiropractor practitioner can help if that is the cause.

If he is simply obsessed with a particular toy and there is no obvious cause you could try weaning him off it by introducing other novel toys. Have a few really interesting interactive ones and rotate them. While he is playing with the new toy, watch to see if the old one is left for a while; can you remove it for a short amount of time before he notices? If this causes distress try getting a number of toys identical to his favourite one: if given all of them, can he swap between the old one and the new one: if he has many, does he still obsess about the original one or can he play with the new ones too?

Pica, Excessive Licking, Polydipsia and Polyphagia

In some cases these behaviours, if not due to a health issue, can stem from an emotional origin so it is really important to calm your dog's environment and reduce any conflict going on. Look at what upsets your dog and see if you can improve or remove the stressor. It is doubly important that dogs with these behaviours are not admonished for these actions, or the emotional response will just worsen and could prompt the behaviour to detcriorate further. Tellington TTouch mouth work is really useful for quietening these behaviours, and of course, look at gut issues to eliminate this as a cause.

In the meantime be vigilant about leaving food or items that can be swallowed around where your dog can get hold of them, provide lots of appropriate items to lick or chew and make sure that water bowls are not empty for too long otherwise your polydipsic dog may become dehydrated and in turn obsess about drinking water even more. To stop him drinking too much try having lots of small water bowls around the house so he has to move between them and break from drinking. This won't work for all dogs but it might stop dogs who drink large amounts then vomit it up, from being sick. Never restrict a dog's water intake unless advised by your vet. Some medical conditions make dogs drink excessive amounts so do talk to your vet about Cushing's disease, kidney failure and Diabetes Mellitus as well as other possible causes.

Conflict

If your dog's behaviour is caused by conflict with another dog or person in the household (maybe you have a baby or toddler that won't leave him alone or a teenager who teases him), look to give him a personal safe space or special time with you. For example, if he doesn't get on well with your other dog, create a safe haven for him or walk him separately, giving him time away from the pressure of the stressful situation. Safe havens don't have to mean a crate or another room. You can easily and cheaply divide rooms with puppy panels so they can see each other but choose to not interact. Even rearranging the furniture so your fearful dog doesn't have to squeeze by the other can make a huge difference.

These simple, and sometimes quick changes can give your dog a positive start on the road to recovery. If there are factors you can't easily change, think about other alterations or management tools you can implement to help your dog cope with the stresses in his life. If you are struggling to come up with creative ways of managing your dog's environment or conflicts within his life contact a qualified behaviourist who can provide a fresh pair of eyes on the situation.

Having made changes to the environment, the next chapter looks at how you can physically manage your dog to help decrease the occurrence of the CCD behaviour or to manage it while you put in place the other training suggestions in this book.

PART FIVE

Equipment and tools to manage your CCD dog

Having considered management of some of the primary environmental triggers, let's now look at some key tools and equipment you can employ to help your dog directly cope with his CCD and give you some respite and peace of mind.

Long line and harness
One management tool some of you may need to use on a walk is a long line. This can be useful for dogs who grab toys away from other dogs, or who dive into ponds to bark and bite at the reflections in the water. Some dogs can do this for hours and be just out of reach, so if you are not prepared to wade in after him, I would suggest using this tool.

Although extending/retractable leashes are a popular choice amongst many owners, a long line can be a safer option which will also enable a greater degree of fine control in its use. The cord on an extending/retractable leash can cause serious injuries to both humans and dogs, and the constant pressure from the mechanism on your dog can set up a pulling action from him, let alone the heaviness in your hand and the worry of not being able to stop him in time in an emergency. If you do apply the brake while your dog is still running, it can also create a horrendous jerk on your dog which may cause injury, and is often forceful enough to pull the handle right out of your hand.

Long lines are available in different lengths, generally 5, 10 and 20 metres (16, 32 and 65 feet) long. They are made in various types of material, but the easiest to manage in terms of use and maintenance are those made of Biothane. This is thin, light, water proof and durable, is highly visible, and has a soft leather-like feel to it.

A long line should always be attached to a harness, never to a collar or head collar. It is recommended that you wear gloves to handle the line, as they will protect your fingers from any injury if it gets pulled through your hand. Driving, sailing or horse-riding gloves are ideal, as they are not too bulky and are non-slip.

When using a long line to exercise your dog you will need to pay attention to it, gathering it in and letting it out as he moves around, and it is also vital that you teach him how to behave while it is attached. You could both sustain injuries for example, should he go zooming off after a squirrel or another dog, so take time to teach him reliable 'stop' and 'steady' commands. If you are unsure how to teach these, book a session with a reputable, qualified dog trainer – details of where to find one are in the Contacts and Resources section.

If your dog has a tendency to spin or chase his tail whilst on leash, then again a harness is advisable so you don't accidently strangle him or damage his neck. A good tip to stop the leash getting twisted up or injuring your hand is to buy a swivel clip if your leash doesn't already have one incorporated into it. Choose one which has a strong ring on the back of it; attach the swivel clip to the harness and the leash to the ring on the back of the clip. When your dog spins the clip will swivel and the leash will stay unsnarled. When the extra clip is used, often dogs stop spinning anyway.

Stroking the leash

If your dog performs an obsessive action whilst on leash, such as digging, trying to grab food off the pavement, or compulsively barking, try employing a Tellington TTouch leading technique called 'stroking the leash'.

This is a great way of regaining his attention and asking him to move away from an area which he is finding distracting, without having to pull at, or wrestle with him.

This can be done while the leash is attached to a flat collar or harness, but not to a check chain or half check. You can even employ this technique on a long line.

To successfully employ this technique you will need a leash which has a smooth surface, such as plain web or leather, rather than one which is plaited, made of chain or with any texture which will make it difficult for your hands to glide easily along it. Some materials may burn your hands as you stroke, especially if your dog needs a firmer, quicker action to respond, so wearing gloves may be a wise safety precaution.

1.

Move out to the side and slightly away from your dog so he can see you in his peripheral vison, and with a little slack in the leash. Hold the leash with both hands. Keeping the end of the leash in your right hand so it doesn't dangle or flap around, move the left hand forwards beneath the leash and take hold of it between forefinger and thumb.

2.
Pause for a moment and then steadily slide your left hand along the leash in a single, continuous movement, from your dog towards you. As your left hand moves closer towards you, the right one moves forwards underneath the leash, takes hold of it between forefinger and thumb, and begins the next stroking movement. Cover around half a metre (one foot) of the leash in each stroking movement.

3.
Each hand repeatedly strokes the same section of the leash in turn: as one finishes a stroke, the other should be starting the next stroking action, moving in a smooth, rhythmical fashion. Think of the movement as starting at your feet – don't plant or brace them, but remain soft and mobile throughout the whole of your body, so you are not just using your arms alone.

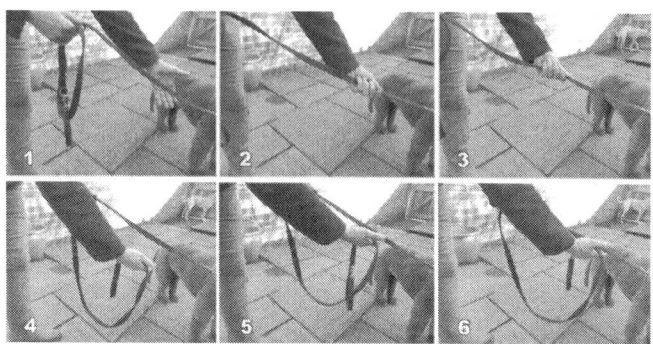

Stroking the leash   *(photo: Toni Shelbourne)*

4.
You may need to try stroking at different speeds or with a varying degree of firmness, but always keep it smooth and try not to drop the connection between you and your dog. If you suddenly allow

the leash to go very slack, it will throw him off balance.

5.
You can also gently call his name and if he starts to move towards you, use the stroking to guide him in the direction you want him to go. You could also reward him at this point with a treat as a reinforcement of the action you wanted. At first you may only get him to look at you for a second before returning to his previous obsession, but be persistent and it will help you move him on. As you get better at the technique and your dog responds more and more to the stroking action on the leash, you will find it easier to prevent previous triggers from stimulating the unwanted behaviour (if you know the antecedent), especially if you can get him focused on you before he starts the negative behaviour. For example, if he barks at traffic and you see a car coming, start the stroking *before* it gets close enough for him to start reacting.

Before trying it out on your dog, it is a good idea to first practise this on a person. This will enable you to refine the technique and develop a smooth action, sustaining a constant even, light tension without jerking or dropping the connection between you as you stroke along the leash.

To practise on a human, either attach the leash to the belt loop of their jeans or ask them to hold one end between their hands. Practice faster and slower stroking and experiment with creating firmer and lighter tensions on the leash with each stroke. Ask for feedback about how it feels, and then swop places, so you can also appreciate what your dog will be feeling, both when you stroke the leash and when you handle it clumsily.

Muzzles

For safety, pica sufferers may need to wear a muzzle while you are getting to the bottom of the problem. Never leave a dog muzzled whilst on his own, and train him to be comfortable wearing one by building up positive associations with it. It may take you up to several weeks before he can wear it with relative ease for longer periods of time. Some dogs will never be truly comfortable with muzzles, so you need to keep up the positivity with them - things like: 'Hey, you get yummy treats when you are wearing it', or 'You get to go for a fab walk', or 'If you wear this for a while, then straight after it comes off you get to play ball or have a favourite game of tuggy with me'.

How to train wearing a muzzle

Muzzles come in a variety of shapes and sizes to suit every different canine face: make sure you buy one which is both the right size and shape for your dog so that it will be a comfortable fit on him as well as being effective. It should also be a basket design, not the fabric type that holds the mouth closed. Dogs can't eat, drink and, more importantly, pant to cool down when wearing the fabric versions.

For dogs who are very concerned about anything on their faces, doing some Tellington Touch body work first, particularly the mouth work (see Part 7), can be a really helpful preparation for muzzle training. Dogs with CCDs often hold a lot of tension in their faces so for many, mouth work is an essential first step.

How many times you need to repeat any of the steps in muzzle training will vary from one dog to another; be patient, and be guided by him. It is always better to over-prepare than not to spend sufficient time on each one, which can result in loss of confidence and set-backs. You can do more than one session a day, but keep each session short and, if he is particularly nervous, give him days off from the muzzle training. The key to muzzle training is not to rush it, and make it fun.

1.
Prepare lots of your dog's favourite soft chewy treats, cut into very small pieces. Hold the muzzle behind your back and call your dog over. As he approaches, bring the muzzle into view and as he investigates it, maybe touching it with his nose, say YES! and give him a treat. Hide the muzzle behind your back again, and throw a treat a short distance away from you so your dog moves away. Repeat this over and over for a maximum of five minutes. Each time he investigates and touches the muzzle, mark it with a YES! and treat. If your dog is struggling with the exercise, ask him to do something familiar and easy such as a sit, or a trick he knows well before going back to the new game. If he loses interest or needs a break, take several breaks during this five minute session for a fun game or some down time.

2.
The next step is to hold the muzzle so the opening faces towards your dog. Don't try to put it on his nose, but do reward lavishly any movement of his nose towards the inside the muzzle which he does voluntarily. End the session after a maximum of five minutes. Repeat this stage as many times as necessary until you think he is ready to move on to the next one.

3.
When your dog is ready to progress further, repeat

steps 1 and 2 a few times, and then try putting a treat inside the muzzle and see if he will reach right in to get the treat out. Remember to give frequent breaks by tossing a treat a short distance away from you, or by asking for another behaviour, such as a trick or obedience exercise he knows well. Repeat this stage over several days or sessions.

4.

You can start to ask him to keep his nose in the muzzle a little longer by feeding him through the holes in the muzzle. You will need to keep the treats coming in quick succession, so have a pile of them in your hand ready to push through the muzzle into his mouth. If he looks uncomfortable and it seems as though he will retreat, quickly take the muzzle away. At this point I often go back to an easier step towards, or in the middle of a training session, so it becomes easier rather than harder for him, for a short time. You will need to carefully judge when you can push forward with training and when you might need to back off. Remember that you are looking for him to voluntarily and happily put his nose in the muzzle. If he looks tentative or hesitates, have a fun break or end the session and go back a stage in the training.

5.

For the next stage, see if you can hold the straps in place behind his ears while repeating step 4 above. You can also do the strap up with the muzzle dangling around his neck to accustom him to the weight and feel - but only try this if it won't panic him.

6.

Once your dog is happy with each of these stages,

you can start adding duration to wearing the muzzle on the face. It is recommended that especially if you have an anxious dog, you initially increase duration with you holding it in place without doing it up, so you can release it quickly. Then return to shorter durations of it actually buckled in place, once you move on to this phase, as you want to avoid him scrabbling at it and trying to pull it off.

Once your dog is comfortable with the muzzle don't assume you can stop rewarding him for wearing it. Regularly associate the muzzle with food and fun to ensure his continued comfort. Some dogs learn to accept wearing muzzles with little anxiety but others never seem to become accustomed to them, so work hard at helping your dog cope.

Crates

A covered crate can be ideal as a management tool for shadow chasers if you find you can't adapt the environment enough, or for times when you are busy and unable to implement training. You can place it in a darker area away from windows, and cover all but the front with a blanket: this will block vision to areas of light that may trigger the behaviour, and will help to encourage your dog to chill out and rest. Take time and forethought in the location of the crate, as you don't want him to feel isolated from you, be in a draught, or in an area that is too busy if he finds it hard to switch off.

Crates should not be used as a place where you put your dog for hours on end as an alternative to working on solving the problem. They should be used sparingly, as a safe or inviting place to go, and never for longer than a couple of hours at a time.

Choose a style of crate suitable for your dog. The

most common and accessible ones are wire framed, but crates are also available in a variety of other materials including fabric, mesh, plastic or you can even buy fancy wooden ones. You may have a preference but it is more important that it is appropriate and safe for your dog. It is no use having a fabric crate for example, if your dog chews, digs or spins as he might chew or dig his way out, or knock it over, as they are lightweight.

The crate must be big enough for your dog to stand up, lie down flat, and comfortably turn around. While in it, he should have access to water, and have a comfy bed on which to snooze or curl up with a long lasting, safe chew.

Not all dogs take to crates, though, and as with muzzle training, you may have to take your time and be patient and imaginative in accustoming your dog to it.

You can introduce it by simply putting it up, placing a comfy bed in there and leaving the door open, and allowing him to investigate it in his own time. You can encourage this by routinely tossing a few tasty treats in there for him to reach in and find, or maybe throwing his favourite toy in there for him to retrieve. You could even place his dinner in the entrance, but watch for any signs of anxiety, such as bolting or not eating his food. If this happens, stop feeding there for the moment and try feeding him outside, next to the crate instead. Continue building up a good association with it by throwing yummy treats into the entrance and then further and further in. Make it fun and take your time. If your dog continues to show anxiety then perhaps try an alternative such as a puppy pen, a den under chairs or a table as explained further below.

If you have a very busy, high drive dog, a great

training gambit is to put lots of his favourite toys, bed and some yummy treats inside the crate, allowing him to see you doing this. Then shut the door – but with him on the outside. This type of dog often begs you to open the door and let him in!

Leave the door open at all times initially, so he can enter and leave when he wants. Only when he is confidently walking in and out of the crate, and maybe even choosing to lie down inside, try shutting it. Pick a time to do this when he is involved with his dinner or a long lasting chew; quietly push the door to, but do not lock it. Stay close by to open it quickly once he has finished, or allow him to push the door open by himself. If he is comfortable with this, then over the next few days you can try locking the door for a few seconds. If he looks worried and he doesn't settle, drop a few more treats in through the bars or gaps if you are able to, and then let him straight out and go back a stage.

Build up the length of time he spends in the crate slowly and carefully. Don't rush this as it is important that he loves the crate, and views it as a place where all good things happen, where it is safe, quiet, and with the comfiest bed in there. It needs to be his retreat, not his prison. The golden rule is that you should always be on hand to monitor his level of comfort. Dogs can cause themselves serious injuries if they panic in a crate, so watch carefully for any signs of distress and act appropriately if he appears concerned.

When you think that he is ready to be left in the crate while you leave the room, slowly build up the amount of time you leave him, just for a minute or two at first. If it is feasible, you could also set up a camera – this will enable you to keep an eye on him from elsewhere in the house, and you can then return promptly if he shows signs of anxiety.

There are several ways you can adapt your home or this idea if you don't have room for a crate or want something less permanent. If, for example, he loves to hide behind furniture or under the table, use a blanket to make it darker and more den-like. As with crate-training, encourage him to settle there with some yummy enrichment such as a chew or stuffed Kong.

Another alternative is to buy puppy pen panels that fit together to create a safe den which is easily put up and taken down and stored away if you don't need it permanently. These are useful for dogs who might also appreciate a little space away from another animal in the house or from small children who haven't yet learnt to leave him alone while he is sleeping. The panels enable you to section off parts of rooms, giving him more space than a crate would do. They are good for dogs that panic in small spaces or for those in whom conflict is a factor in their CCD, as it creates a barrier and gives them peace of mind and respite from the stress. If you search for puppy pen panels on the internet you will find lots of places selling them, and offering a variety of heights if you have a bigger dog. Of course this option isn't safe for dogs who might jump out as injury might occur.

If you are good at DIY a further option might be to convert a suitable area in your house to create a safe haven for your CCD dog. I have seen some fabulous under-stairs spaces converted to indoor kennels – you will find lots of ideas online to get your creative juices flowing.

Veterinary collars for flank suckers or obsessive lickers

If your dog is self-harming with excessive licking,

whilst you are getting to the root of the problem and putting in some changes and training, you may have to resort to a veterinary collar to prevent serious injury. This doesn't have to be the traditional plastic conical shaped versions you often get from the vets if your dog has stitches; you can now buy some great and comfortable alternatives, ranging from inflatable doughnut-shaped ones to foam or cloth versions which are easier for your dog to cope with. Do an internet search for veterinary or recovery collars and you will find plenty of alternatives.

This may or may not work for tail chasers, but might stop him causing quite so much damage to the limb, while for excessive pica sufferers this might be an alternative to a muzzle. For both issues, the cone would need to be long enough and sturdy enough for him not to be able to reach the object of his desire. As always, take time accustoming your dog to wearing it; you can use the same principles as for muzzle training (see above).

Whatever the CCD, there will be a piece of equipment or a tool that works for you – be prepared to get creative and think outside the box. It is crucial to bear in mind that these suggestions are *not* a fix for the problem, just a temporary means of helping to manage it while you change whatever needs to be changed. You will still need to find that underlying health issue responsible and seek treatment for it, or to work through the problem with training and changes to your dog's lifestyle.

Now you've calmed your dog's environment and found some management tools to help you stay sane and your dog stay safe, it's time to look at ways that might help you to change the behaviour for good...

PART SIX

Mental stimulation and enrichment

There are many ways in which you can enrich your dog's life with appropriate mental stimulation. This is essential for all dogs, not just those who obsess about something. Vigorous physical exercise is not always the best way to tire out a dog – twenty minutes of throwing a ball in the park for him to chase can actually stimulate him to be more hyperactive; it can also end up with him being seriously injured. Swap that twenty minutes of ball throwing for scent work, and you will be amazed not only by how much your dog enjoys it, but how much it will tire him too.

Nowadays there are so many enrichment toys available for sale that you could easily spend a small fortune on them. In this chapter, though, I will concentrate on some inexpensive, homemade alternatives you can try, plus suggesting some training ideas and activities you can do with your active dog. If you can aim to include at least twenty to thirty minutes of mental stimulation on top of your dog's daily walks you may find that he becomes a lot calmer. Choose tasks you will both enjoy, such as teaching him fun tricks or using his nose. Should you get stuck for ideas you'll find plenty of inspiration on YouTube – there are any number of clips which will show you how to train cool tricks that will wow your friends and calm your pooch. Working with a qualified trainer would also give you further appropriate ideas, and there are some good books listed in the Further Reading section.

From the observations you completed earlier in the book, you will know when your dog is most active, so try to sync with this period if you can. For example, because I know my dog is at his most active first thing in the morning and between 13.00 and 15.00 in the afternoon I schedule my day to fit around these peak activity times. This might not be possible for everyone but as far as you are able to, try and fit in with his natural daily rhythm. Although it is sometimes counter-productive to stick to rigid timetables, for some dogs it is a necessary evil; the trick, as always, is to know your dog and his individual needs. If you do need to change his routine, try and do it slowly.

Exercise

'A happy dog is a tired dog', is a saying you tend to hear a lot. This is not always true, but certainly if your dog is bored, under-exercised and under-stimulated he is much more likely to go 'self-employed', i.e. come up with a way of occupying himself. I am not suggesting that you get your running shoes on and take him for a five mile jog every day (although some dogs might need this, in which case taking up Canicross might be worth thinking about). The amount of exercise needs to match your dog's age, breed, fitness and energy levels; try increasing exercise a little at a time so you build fitness together. Keep a daily dog diary, and make a note of when his rest cycle lengthens and if his CCD decreases with the extra physical activity. Don't have time? Then think about employing a dog walker for some days of the week, or else make a vow that you will get up half an hour earlier to walk him before work.

One word of warning, if your dog is nervous or hyperactive, fast exercise will increase adrenaline and could exacerbate the problem; moderate or slow exercise on the other hand, increases serotonin levels in the brain, which will help him to relax more. Don't therefore, be tempted to simply do a lot more ball throwing, as far from improving matters, it might actually make things worse.

Exercise also needs to be mentally stimulating, and fun for your dog. This means satisfying some of his doggy requirements like sniffing a tree for five minutes so he can pick up all his 'pee mail', or having a play date with a friendly dog he gets on with. A route march around the block with no time for investigating anything is not going to cut it either physically or mentally for a young, active dog.

Enriching walks
There are plenty of ways you can make walks more interesting and fun, so that you stimulate your dog's mind as well as tiring him physically. Too often, we pay little attention to our dogs once we unclip the leash. Consequently, they often think it is their time to do whatever they wish, and this can get some individuals into trouble. It is also very easy to fall into the habit of going to the same place and following the same route on every walk.

Take your dog somewhere different for a change, watch how much he uses his nose to work his way through the new environment, and then notice how tired he is when you get home. If it isn't possible to visit new places, then vary how you walk your route: do it backwards, or take a zig zag approach, and go and investigate any new objects in the environment such as large rocks or fallen tree branches. Even walking to the park via a different route or along the other side of the road can bring new sights and smells to stimulate your dog's senses.

If you are road walking, try walking really slowly, so your dog is encouraged to sniff as much as he likes. You can even let him pick the route; dogs love to be able to track interesting scents, so facilitate this by being a follower every so often.

Going for a walk is also a brilliant opportunity to engage with your dog and play with him - make him believe you are the best thing in the park! Most dogs enjoy getting the chance to put their powerful sense of smell to work with the following very simple scenting games you can play with him:

Find it!
Take a handful of tasty treats or a few of your dog's favourite toys. Drop a treat or a toy in the grass or a safe area of undergrowth and ask your dog to sniff it out. Make it very easy for him at first, but as he gets used to, and more skilled at the game you can make it harder by making the treat more difficult to find. Once he is good at it, you can also vary it by throwing multiple treats for him to seek out.

What's this?
If your dog isn't paying you much attention, drop a treat on the floor, and then point to it saying 'What's this?' in an excited tone of voice. When your dog discovers you are brilliant at foraging, he will stick to you like glue.

Track it!
Leave your dog in a sit/stay, or if the temptation is going to be too great for him to maintain it, ask a

friend to hold him while you lay a short trail of really tasty and smelly treats. Let him see them in your hand and watch you lay the trail: as you move away from him keep bending over to touch the ground, sometimes putting a treat down and sometimes not. Place the treats at close distances to start with, and in a straight line. As your dog gets better at sniffing out and following the trail, start spacing them further apart. You can make it more difficult by zigzagging rather than moving in a straight line so he has to really use his nose and be thorough to find them all.

The treats you use must be yummy enough to be motivating for your dog, or the toy a firm favourite. If you aren't having much luck in getting him interested, then the toys or treats need to be higher value: if it needs to be steak, then it needs to be steak! If your dog shows a talent for scenting and tracking, you'll find the book *Smellorama! Nose Games for Your Dog* by Viviane Theby excellent (*see Further Reading*).

You can also use objects in the environment to fire your dog's interest; ask him to jump over or walk along logs, weave between bollards, crawl under benches - anything which gets him to improve his body awareness, and which is safe, fun and enriching. The time out together can be used to refine some of your basic obedience too; practise recalls, walking to heel, down stays, and waits, but always make it pleasurable and rewarding. If you are enjoying it, he will too. It needn't take up too much time; ten minutes in the middle of your walk can be enough. Intersperse it with plenty of fun games or some retrieves.

Dog activities to enrich your dog's life
Try and tailor activities to your dog's breed and the

purpose he was bred for; for example, Labradors love to retrieve, Huskies to run, Bloodhounds want to track, and collies to herd. See if you can tap into his natural instincts in a safe, modern way to satisfy his need to perform the task he was bred for. This may, of course, not be possible on a walk but there are many activities you can get involved in with your dog these days which you will both enjoy. The key as always, is picking something your dog will instinctively enjoy and excel at. Below is a list with a brief description of some of the more popular and accessible activities:

Agility: Running around a course with your dog, directing him over and through obstacles.

Bikejoring: Cycling with your dog.

Canicross: Running with your dog.

Competition obedience: Obedience done in a highly stylised manner.

Disc Dog: Fun with Frisbees.

Flyball: A team sport where dogs run a short course, collect a ball and return to their handler, done as a relay race with a team of dogs and handlers.

Gundog training or working field trials: Gundog work where dogs and handlers compete against each other. There are also plenty of pet dog gundog training available now too, and it isn't necessary to be involved in the blood sport.

Heel work to Music: Dog and handler perform a routine to music.

Parkour: Using natural obstacles in your environment to encourage your dog to jump, balance and climb.

Rally-O: A sport involving obedience exercises where you and your dog complete a course with various tasks on the way.

Sledding & mushing: One or more dogs pull a

sled, or are harnessed to a three-wheeled 'rig' that looks like a chariot when there is no snow.
Tracking: Dogs follow a scent trail. Other scent work involves detection work.
Treibball: A sport where dogs have to push large exercise balls towards the handler and through a goal.
Trick Training: Learning fun tricks with your dog.

There are many local clubs or trainers that offer these activities, and it is a great way of meeting new people, too.

Garden activities
If you have a garden, you can utilize it during good weather to offer some tiring and fun enrichment for your dog.
Scatter feed:
The simplest and cheapest fun activity is a scatter feed in the grass. You can use part or all of your dog's dinner if he is fed kibble; just throw it out over a wide area and ask him to go find it. This can keep some dogs amused for ages if they enjoy using their nose but if yours gives up easily, scatter a little less, spread out over a smaller area so it is not wasted and encourages vermin.

If you feed raw or tinned meat, you can still scatter feed; adapt it by gathering together lots of small bowls, putting a spoonful of food in each and then hiding them in and around those areas of the garden where you don't mind your dog exploring. He may need help at first but once he gets the idea, he will be racing around having fun hunting out his dinner and tiring himself out both physically and mentally in the process. Alternative food items to spread around might include small chewy treats, such as pieces of cooked cubed liver or chicken, hotdog, cheese ... anything your dog loves and which is safe and good for him. My dog adores having a tin of tuna scattered in the grass - it takes forever to find all the tiny bits!

The cup game:
Buy some cheap picnic bowls and cups: place them upside down with a treat hidden under each one. Ask your dog to seek the treats out; he may need help at first to work out how to knock the cups and bowls over in order to reach the treat, but as he becomes more adept you can increase the difficulty by stacking the cups up with treats in each layer.

You can also place them further apart so he has to physically move, too; this is great for dogs who are very busy. Keep refilling the pots and cups; you will see him slowing down as he tires; after ten to twenty minutes of this activity, many dogs are often exhausted. If your dog isn't very food orientated, try hiding his favourite toys instead.

The treasure box:
The treasure box is another good, long lasting

enrichment game which is cheap and easy to do. Get a large cardboard box – it will need to be big enough for lots of other boxes and toys to fit into, but of an appropriate size for your dog.

Save up empty tissue boxes, egg cartons, cereal and other food boxes, and the inner cardboard tubes from toilet and kitchen towel rolls. You might also save plain packing paper. Be careful about using newspaper if you think your dog might consume it, both because of possible chemicals in the ink or bleach on the paper, and to avoid it causing a blockage in his digestive tract. As an alternative, use towels instead. Gather together lots of treats, toys and chews, both big and small, with varying levels of yumminess. Hide the food (which can be part or all of his dinner) in the boxes, wrapped loosely inside pieces of paper or the towels, add in a chew or two and some favourite toys. Put the box somewhere you can see and supervise, but basically let your dog work it out. It will take a good length of time to find all the 'treasure' and consume or play with them all. If he finishes it too quickly, you evidently have a genius on your hands, so try making the puzzles harder!

The muffin tin game:
There are many other enrichment games you can make: the muffin tin game is often a great favourite. Take a muffin tin, and drop a small treat in a few or all of the indents. Place a tennis ball on top of each indent. Your dog will have to sniff out the treats, and then move the balls in order to reach them. Some dogs get clever and just tip up the tray but the game can work well for smaller, less exuberant dogs.

If the muffin game is too easy, buy a pack of ball pit balls (these are very cheap) and a container to put them in. This could be an old car tyre, a sturdy, non-slip children's paddling pool with an added non-slip mat in the bottom for safety, a wooden box - anything that is large and heavy enough not to tip up and scare or injure him. Place the balls in the pit; if he is ball-obsessed this will be enough in itself, but if he prefers food, throw in some treats for him to rummage around for.

Summer day entertainment

If your dog is a digger, you may find the ball pit is enough to entertain him if you keep hiding treats and toys in there for him to find but if he habitually digs up your flower beds, why not create a digging pit just for him? These can be as cheap or expensive as you want, and depending upon your level of DIY skills you can build one from scratch, use ready-made clip-together raised bed panels, or a rigid plastic child's paddling pool, which can then be filled with clean top soil. You can find more details on making a digging pit, and how to encourage your dog to use it in *Help! My Dog is Destroying the Garden* (*see Further Reading*) as well as online. One important tip: cover it when not in use so that the local cats and wildlife don't use it as a toilet!

Ice lollies can be fun to make and are a great way to keep your dog cool and entertained on hot summer days. It is easy to make up a batch and store them in the freezer, and you don't need any fancy moulds, as an empty, clean plastic takeaway container is good enough. Use your dog's favourite treats, and you can even make the ice more appealing by using meaty stock. It's cooling, messy and fun for your dog to devour – although don't give him multiple lollies on the same day, in case it upsets his stomach.

If your dog isn't very keen on ice, but loves fruit and veg you can make edible treat toys instead out of things such as cored apples or carrots. Cut out small holes, remove any pith or seeds that may be harmful if indigestible, and refill with a mix of yummy food. You will find plenty of other ideas and recipes on the internet generally as well as specifically on Facebook pages such as 'Beyond the Bowl – Canine Enrichment' for lots of enriching fun. (*See also Further Reading*).

Chews

Some dogs need to chew, especially if they are emotional, sensitive creatures. A good dose of daily, appropriate, supervised chewing can be very beneficial - even essential - for some, with the act of chewing helping to promote the release of calming endorphins. The sort of chewing you want to encourage is slow, deliberate, steady, satisfying gnawing, rather than rapid, destructive, trying-to-swallow-chunks type of activity. Always supervise your dog when you give him long lasting items to chew, as you don't want him swallowing large, indigestible parts which might cause a blockage.

If you can't give your dog raw bones regularly there are many safe alternatives. Some dogs who destroy normal chews in minutes might enjoy root-based chews or the coffee-wood chew which is now available. These wood based chew toys don't splinter and are really safe for all but the most excessively hard chewer.

No bone or chew is completely without risk of causing problems internally. Know your dog and choose your chew with care after researching it thoroughly, especially if your dog has health issues, tends to put weight on (some have a high fat content), or a history of swallowing items whole, as pica suffers might. Steer clear of cheap highly-coloured substances and check the label carefully if your dog has allergies; you may be surprised at how many treats contain chicken, a food many dogs are intolerant of. Avoid nylon-type bones too as these can be toxic and also become very sharp, causing injury to the gums; and be careful with the harder chews like antlers if he is an extreme chewer as these can damage the teeth, as can large hard, weight bearing raw bones like knuckle bones.

There are many interactive food toys, and products such as slow feeders and lick mats on the market; but while it can be wise to invest some money and buy a few, as you can see it need not cost you the earth and you can get really creative with your ideas. Your dog will be occupied, happy and mentally stimulated.

Brain Training

For the Einsteins of the dog world who are super-intelligent you might have to investigate activities that assess his cognitive skills. There is an online test you can do called Dognition which can give you some idea as to what level of genius your dog is, while working his brain at the same time as you go through the various exercises. It is not very expensive to do and can be really fun for both of you.

You might also like to look up the training system *Do As I Do*, which showcases your dog's social cognitive skills. Created by Claudia Fugazza, this method teaches your dog to copy your actions and can demonstrate that dogs can retain instructions for a long time after they have been shown (*see also Further Reading*).

Many good dog trainers teach cognitive skills, so find someone local to guide you through pattern recognition exercises, such as identifying a shape or colour or learning the names of toys. It is fascinating to see how clever dogs are: my dog can play noughts and crosses, picking out the O and X shapes when asked. As it can be mentally tiring too, it doesn't take long to satisfy him and it's a great party piece to show off to friends when they visit.

Real Dog Yoga
Another brilliant training method you can try with your dog is Real Dog Yoga. Not only is it fun and mentally stimulating, it will promote calm thoughtfulness too, which can make all the difference to a dog showing CCD-like symptoms. Unlike Doga, which encourages owners to place their dogs in positions alongside their yoga stances, Real Dog Yoga is a training programme designed to teach dogs postures, actions and expressions which will help them in their daily life. The 30 postures, 10 expressions and 15 actions promote calmness through stimulating the parasympathetic nervous system, and encouraging body awareness, muscle control and communication skills. Created by Jo-Rosie Haffenden (from the popular TV programmes *Rescue Dog to Super Dog* and *Teach My Pet To Do That*), Real Dog Yoga promotes option training, a way for your dog to opt in or out of learning. This is done by using a yoga mat. When on the mat you are training but when your dog steps off it you stop; this gives him the choice to continue, break for a rest, or stop altogether. It has been shown that dogs (and humans), take on information much more readily and retain the information if sessions are short and breaks are frequent.

Real Dog Yoga trains dogs using a clicker, (a small

training aid which gives a specific sound) or a marker word like YES. This technique tells your dog when he has accomplished the desired behaviour; the click or word tells him if he is getting it right or is heading in the right direction, and the desired action is reinforced with a food reward. A click means food, and he will try to get you to click/feed again by repeating the action he believed earned him the food. In this way you can shape the action, expression or posture you are looking for.

The contract you make with him, however, is that if he steps off the mat, he is taking a break from training and is encouraged to go play, have a cuddle with you, or go off for a sniff around the garden, and if he doesn't return to the mat, to call an end to training for that session. At first your dog may need to be taught to take breaks if he is a keen worker, by you taking him off to do other things like play with a toy or have a cuddle, or whatever your dog loves to do best.

Once he is more experienced at the training, and through you being disciplined and stopping the training each time he looks as though he is losing interest, your dog learns that he has a choice. If he leaves the mat, and indicates that he doesn't want to participate in training by returning to it, respect this and stop the session. Often dogs very quickly fly back to the mat but they can be different on different days. Watch out for signs from him that he has had enough. These may include looking elsewhere, sniffing the ground, yawning or licking his nose; listen to him and take a break. Encourage him to drink or play, and take a drink yourself. Like all activities that use our brains, 20 minutes is a good amount of time to spend doing training but some dogs will need less and some will ask for more. If, after a break you invite him back on to the mat and he still displays these signs, then it is definitely time to stop. Real Dog Yoga is about working with your dog, not making him work.

As with human yoga, ask for each action, expression or posture to be executed mindfully. This means slowing every action down or holding the posture for longer. When movements are slowed and held, you can stretch the body and help the mind to calm. Dogs taught Real Dog Yoga are often witnessed repeating the actions, postures or expressions in their everyday life, i.e. the act of lying down with his head on his feet or crossing his paws encourages restfulness. These life skills are perfect for boisterous Labradors or hyper Huskies, but any breed of dog, and all life stages, can benefit from the training. Real Dog Yoga can be taught indoors, in the garden or anywhere your dog would normally start performing his compulsive behaviour.

Getting started
To gct startcd, you will need:
- A yoga mat
- A clicker
- Lots of treats
- A bowl of water for your dog
- A glass of water for you
- A favourite toy or play area like a ball pool
- Access to a comfy bed
- Two pots: one will be a 'non-active' pot which contains the bulk of your treats and is reserved for later in the session. The other pot will be the 'active' one, used to hold the treats you will count out to work with. Alternatively you can use a treat bag if you prefer. Counting out treats will remind you to take a break and means you

don't have to remember how many repetitions have been done of a certain action.

A note on treats - medium or high value treats will mean different things to different dogs. If you are a Labrador, even boring kibble is high value! Have a variety of treats pre-cut into small workable pieces. Try not to use anything that is too messy on your fingers. Sometimes if a treat is too tasty it distracts from the task being taught; however, other dogs might need something really high value to motivate them to try.

It is best if the treats are chewy rather than crunchy so your dog doesn't choke or spend a lot of time chewing. Also you may use a lot, and for safety reasons, you don't want your dog to eat a large amount of kibble. Tempting treats to use include cocktail sausages, hotdogs, liver cake, small chunks of cooked heart or kidney, healthy, soft chewy small commercial training treats, cooked chicken, ham, etc; choose something that you know won't upset your dog's stomach. It is also worth noting that training your dog just after his meal might not be the best option – if he is a little peckish, he will be far more motivated than when he is full and sleepy.

Each dog will differ in the length of time he can concentrate for, but be prepared to take lots of breaks; in fact if he doesn't take them naturally, then encourage him to take a breather by having a game with his favourite toy, going outside for toileting, or taking time for a cuddle - but somewhere else, not on the mat. The mat is only for when you are working.

If you haven't worked with a clicker before, take time to practise before training so you are comfortable using it; make sure you do this out of earshot of your dog. Timing is everything in clicker training so that you can pinpoint the exact moment your dog performs the desired action. If your timing is not very good, it can result in you clicking an action you don't want, which can end up confusing your dog. Get your eye in and sharpen up your reaction time by practising with a tennis ball; bounce the ball - can you click the precise moment every time it hits the ground?

Even if your dog is used to a clicker, spend some time reintroducing it. If he is sound sensitive either make the click quieter by muffling the sound in your pocket or use a word instead. Click and then immediately feed your dog a small tasty treat. Repeat this until you can see that your dog is anticipating getting a treat each time he hears the click.

Introducing the mat

Once the clicker is his new best friend, lay the mat out. He will probably immediately go to investigate it; as soon as he steps on to the mat, click and treat. If he doesn't, throw a treat on it to encourage him to step on or use a treat held in your hand to lure him.

If he remains on the mat you can encourage him to get off again by throwing another treat a small distance away. When he returns, repeat the click and treat when he steps on the mat. Do this until you can see he knows the mat is where all the good stuff happens.

Try to get him to stand squarely on the mat. To encourage this, stand at one of the short sides and throw the treat directly away from you off the other short end. Your dog will then naturally return straight on and you can reward for four feet on the mat, which is what you want *(overleaf)*.

Once your dog understands that the mat is the

Introducing the mat *(photo: Toni Shelbourne)*

place to be, you can start to introduce a base position. This is either a stand, sit or down.

Choose whichever your dog is most comfortable with initially; as you advance you can introduce the others. Because you want your dog to start to slow down, encourage him to hold the stand, sit or down for three of your own slow breaths.

You may have to work up to this extended period – at first you will have to click and treat after just one breath, building up to two, and finally for three. It may take you a whole session, just to practise that. Observe his breathing; does it start to slow, does his body soften, can he remain focused on you, waiting patiently for the reward?

Once you have reached this point, you will then be ready to start teaching him some posture training. A few simple postures are included here to start you off; to find out more see Jo-Rosie Haffenden's book *The Real Dog Yoga* - details are in the Further Reading section.

- ***Head turns***

This posture can be taught in the stand, sit or down position and is excellent for stretching out a tight neck or encouraging dogs to look away from something.

1.
Begin by reintroducing the clicker and the mat, and then settle your dog in the base position of his choice; remember to get him to hold it for three breaths.

2.
Count out 10 treats and place them in your active pot or treat bag, ready for use. Every time your dog makes any movement with his head to the side *(pic A overleaf)*, click (or use your marker word) and treat. At first you may need to encourage him to do this by luring him with a treat held to the side in your hand; or you might try looking in that direction yourself, or get someone to make a small noise or movement to prompt the action. It is best to pick a head turn to one side only, so as not to confuse him for now. Later on you can teach him to turn his head to the other side.

3.
Shape this behaviour so that each time he moves his head you ask him for a little bit more *(pic B overleaf)*. Repeat until you have done 9 repetitions

Head turns: pic A *(photo: Toni Shelbourne)*

and then on the 10th, throw the treat off of the mat to give your dog a chance to relax.

4.
Count out 10 more treats and repeat. With each repetition try to give him less help, to test if he understands what the reward is being dispensed for. Eventually you will only treat the furthest turns

Head Turns: pic B *(photo: Toni Shelbourne)*

of his head, and then reward the longest ones. Note that this will take several sessions, possibly over a few days or even a week, depending on how easily your dog learns.

5.
Once he consistently offers the head turn you can start to name it. As he looks in that direction, say 'Stretch left' (or right, depending on which side you

have been working on). Remember to break often, giving him time to take a drink, (and take a drink yourself), and to do something else. Some dogs need more breaks and/or a longer duration of break, while others need to be encouraged to rest. This posture will not be perfected in a day, so keep working at it. Once he has learned it, you can start to introduce the head turn to the other side.

Note: If your dog is elderly, or stiff due to holding tension or from a neck injury, do not do too many repetitions as you could make him sore. Think about how you feel yourself when you return to the gym or an exercise class after a break - you can really feel the after-effects for a few days, and that will be just how he will feel too, so be gentle and considerate. If you are worried about overdoing things, count out the maximum number of treats you want to use for the whole of your training session in to your non-active pot so when they are all gone you know it is time to stop and go have some fun elsewhere with him.

- *Head on paws (Sad)*

If you would like your dog to chill out, then teaching him to lie down with his head on his paws can be really beneficial as it can be hugely relaxing.

1.

First of all encourage your dog to hold the 'down' base position for three breaths. Once this has been achieved, count out 10 treats.

2.

Take a treat in your closed hand and hold it on the floor between your dog's front paws. Click and treat every time your dog's nose comes down to your hand/floor to investigate, feeding him from the *other* hand **not** the one on the floor.

3.
After a break, count out 15 treats and again ask for a 'down' encouraging him to be calm by rewarding for mindfulness and concentration on you. This time do not have a treat in your hand, but hold it level with his nose, and then point or bring your pointed finger down to the ground and say 'Sad'. Wait for any movement towards the floor with his head and click and treat. Shape this so you begin to only reward the bigger movements, until eventually your dog places his head between his paws and rests it on the floor, or on his paws *(pic C, overleaf)*. Take a break. You may need to repeat these stages several times if your dog is struggling.

4.
By this stage your dog should know that you expect calmness, and understand about base positions. If he is still getting excited, go back to asking for three breaths of stillness, or reduce the value of your treats. Count out 10 treats and when in a 'down', point to the floor and say 'Sad'. Once he consistently does this, start to delay clicking by a fraction of a second at a time so you gradually increase the duration of time he spends lying with his head on the floor or resting on his paws. If he breaks the 'sad' don't reward him; just ask for it again. This time ask for a little less so he can achieve what you are asking - you don't want him becoming frustrated or confused. Remember, this should be fun for both of you!

Real Dog Yoga really does encourage hyperactive dogs to self-soothe and offer different behaviours, which if he is usually inclined to be a bit manic or stressed could really make a difference. If you enjoyed teaching your dog these two exercises, you can find out more by reading the book or attending

Head on paws: pic C *(photo Toni Shelbourne)*

a workshop or class – you'll find details in the Contacts and Resources and Further Reading sections.

Training
Other useful training exercises that might help your dog to stop or limit his compulsive actions are teaching a 'go settle command' and having a

positive interrupter, although both these may be limited in their success until you have worked through the suggestions in Part Seven.

Settle command

A settle command can be very useful if you see your dog just starting to think about going into his behaviour or becoming aroused. However, it might not work once he is in full swing if he doesn't know the command well enough for it to be an automatic response yet, so work on this command every day when he isn't chasing his tail or pouncing on shadows. It is easiest to teach him to go settle on a cosy bed or in his crate where he is more likely to remain and be comfortable.

There are many ways to teach a settle, but basically lure your dog on to a bed or mat and once on, feed him a treat. Once he is consistently walking on to the mat ask for a down, and feed. Don't be mean with the treats! You can continue to feed him in rapid succession to begin with so he enjoys lying on the mat. After a while you can throw a treat from a distance on to the mat, and as he approaches, ask for a down. As he lies down say 'Settle' and throw another treat.

Release him from the mat before he gets up and moves away himself, but each time you repeat the exercise see if he can stay a little longer. You can encourage this by giving him a longer lasting treat on the bed. You can also capture the settle, (this is a training term for using what a dog does naturally as a way of introducing a command). Every time you see him going to his bed to rest, say your settle command. If you are unsure about how to achieve the settle you will find lots of tips and videos on YouTube, or you could ask a qualified trainer to help you.

Positive interrupter

A positive interrupter, if taught right, can help distract a dog from a highly aroused activity such as a compulsive behaviour. You will, however, need to train this thousands of times while he is calm, and then a thousand more times when he is just mildly distracted before you have a chance of hoping it will work when he is fully aroused.

Pick a word to use, one which he doesn't hear often, such as 'calm' or 'enough' or 'hey'. Always say this word in a bright happy voice. This cue should only be used for interrupting his compulsive behaviour, never for anything else. If it is related only to this circumstance, it is easier to get a higher success rate.

1.

Teach your dog the cue at a time when he is relaxed. Say the word you have chosen and feed him a yummy treat. Repeat this as many times a day as you can. If you do one or two repetitions randomly throughout the day you will be able to see if your dog understands that this means a treat is coming.

2.

Start to say your interrupter word and reward when your dog is mildly distracted. At first you will need to go up to him and show him the treat; lure him towards you and feed. As he becomes quicker and more reliable in his response, you can begin repeating the same process when he is in a slightly higher state of arousal.

3.

Try to determine what happens, and what your dog does just before he goes into his compulsive behaviour; you can then use your chosen word and reward to try and prevent the behaviour from developing into a full-blown episode. As before, you will have to start by going right up to him to lure him to you, but eventually he should move towards you when you say the cue. Once you have reached this point in your training, it may work when he is actually performing the behaviour - but don't expect it to work without first achieving a high rate of success in the previous steps, or to be able to stop the behaviour if you haven't also put in any of the other work suggested in this book.

Once you have successfully interrupted the behaviour you will then need to do something to prevent him from returning to it once he has eaten the yummy treat. This is where Tellington TTouch can be extremely beneficial; the next chapter explains why and how to apply it. There are also suggestions for other holistic options which may help diminish or change your dog's behaviour.

PART SEVEN

Finding methods to support your CCD dog and influence behavioural changes for the better

As you can see from the previous chapters you can manage compulsive symptoms in your dog: hopefully, with increased exercise, enrichment, and management of his environment and interactions with us and other species, their frequency will start to decrease.

But what about finding a way to further reduce, or change the behaviour completely? This depends on many factors, including:

- How you deal with the behaviour and handle your dog.
- Your understanding of why it is happening.
- The relationship between you and your dog.
- The reason your dog is displaying the behaviour.
- Any underlying causes, such as health issues or environmental stresses.

It is always worth exploring every avenue to improve your dog's quality of life and keep your sanity. One highly rewarding and successful way of changing a dog's behaviour is through the Tellington TTouch Method, and I have successfully used this training method to help a number of CCD suffers.

The Tellington TTouch Method ®
Devised nearly forty years ago by Linda Tellington Jones, and developed in conjunction with her sister Robyn Hood, Tellington TTouch is often confused with massage. It is actually very different, and as well as the special 'TTouches' (body work) employs a varied system of exercises which include groundwork, equipment and body wraps.

The Tellington TTouch Method - or TTouch® (pronounced Tee Touch) for short – has a proven track record for helping animals with a wide range of issues, including compulsive behaviours and other stress-related problems. It is a kind, non-invasive, generally well accepted and empathic way of working with animals which is easy to learn, simple and safe to apply, and can have profound effects on the lives of animals and on the people who care for them.

The Tellington TTouch Method is based on the principle that posture and behaviour are incxtricably linked, with posture affecting behaviour and vice versa. By improving posture, balance and movement, beneficial physical, psychological and emotional changes are produced, with self-confidence and self-control increasing. Mind and body begin to work together in harmony, and unwanted behaviours diminish or disappear entirely. This is not some far-fetched or whimsical theory, but one which has been successfully demonstrated time and time again, both with Tellington TTouch and in other modalities which focus on posture, such as Alexander Technique.

TTouch provides you with the tools to make changes for the better to your dog's posture – and because tension through the head, neck, back and tail contributes to compulsive behaviours and is often seen in dogs which suffer from them, it can be very successful as part of the remedy.

'Reading' your dog
It is often forgotten just how closely connected posture and behaviour are, even though we constantly use phrases such as having cold feet, gritting our teeth, or tearing our hair out to describe states of mind. We can also perceive how someone is feeling by observing their posture: a happy person will literally be 'standing tall', walking with a bounce in their step, head up and quite possibly a smile on their face. Conversely a depressed person will appear to be drooping, hunched up, with rounded shoulders and a slower, dragging stride.

Just as body language can reflect a state of mind, so the reverse can be true, with poor posture or the presence of 'tension patterns' directly influencing the mental and emotional processes and dictating behaviour.

Dogs with physical and/or behavioural issues frequently exhibit tension patterns. These can develop for a variety of reasons, including physical injury, health issues, frightening experiences, stress and emotional trauma. The tension produced and sustained in specific areas of the body promotes different responses; for example, a dog that holds tension through the head and neck are often seemingly in a state of high alert or hyperactive – these individuals can also suffer from CCD.

Tension patterns show up in many ways. There may be a very hot or cold area on the body: the skin may feel stiff and immobile rather than sliding freely across the underlying tissues: changes in coat colour or texture may be seen, or greasy or dry scurfy patches: swirls and changes of direction in the way the hairs grow may be noticed. Muscling and wear and tear on the nails and pads may differ from one side to the other ... It is a fascinating study, and as you learn to look at your dog in more detail, you will learn a lot about him which can make it easier to help him. More detailed information on tension patterns and how to identify them can be found in Sarah Fisher's book *Unlock Your Dog's Potential* (see *Further Reading*).

Observing your dog is an important part of TTouch work, but it will also benefit you in all other areas of your relationship; noting your dog's posture, how he moves and responds to his environment and the situations he finds himself in will tell you a lot about how he is feeling physically and provide an invaluable key to his mental processes and emotional state.

Learning to 'read' your dog's posture will help you to decide which TTouches to use and where to use them: when to start, and when to stop: and help ensure that you stay safe. You may need to exercise care when handling or performing TTouches on areas which hold a lot of tension, as your dog may be reluctant for you to touch him there, and it may even cause him discomfort when you do. Always keep this latter point in mind, and do read carefully through the section on safety.

Tellington TTouch Body Work: The TTouches

The special 'TTouches' involve gently moving the skin in various ways. They are the foundation of the Tellington TTouch Method and provide a positive way of calming and reassuring, helping your dog to relax, releasing tension and lowering his stress levels. Anyone can do them, no specialised knowledge of anatomy is needed, and they can be used either on their own, in conjunction with other modalities, or with Tellington TTouch equipment such as body wraps (explained further on).

You can learn how to do the TTouches by reading a book, watching a video, attending a workshop or demo, or asking a practitioner to visit (details can be found in the Contacts & Resources, and Further Reading section), and once the basic skills are learnt you can apply them anywhere, anytime, whenever your pet has need of them. It takes only a short time to learn how to produce a beneficial effect, although the more you practise, the better you will become at it.

The TTouches will help your dog to calm his compulsion by developing his self-confidence, self-control and balance. Introduce them at first when your dog is calm so the work is familiar, pleasurable and reassuring to him, and you are at ease about doing them. The TTouches may help him break off performing a compulsive behaviour or stop him going into a cycle but your safety comes first. Do not touch him if he is likely to react in an aggressive manner towards you. Regular sessions when he is not spinning or tail chasing etc should reduce the likelihood of the behaviour occurring so remember to work with him often when he is calm. You may then start to notice that the intensity of the behaviour begins to decrease or you are able to divert him more easily if he begins to perform the action. Introducing the body work when he is at ease will help both of you be more successful, and when his stress level does go up, you will be able to settle him more quickly.

While you are changing his environment and increasing exercise and enrichment (see Parts four, five and six) try and do some TTouches with your dog every day for around ten to twenty minutes in duration, or whenever you can fit a few minutes in, so that it is a normal part of your routine. Once you are confident in performing the TTouches and he is more familiar with them, you can begin to use them to help stop him going into the compulsive behaviour if he starts to show signs of moving into the sequence. Of course, extreme caution should be taken if he displays any aggressive tendencies at this juncture. (Make sure you read the section on safety further down). Each dog is different, so you need to make a risk assessment as to if and when you employ the body work. Your safety comes first. If you are unsure how he will react, distract him from the behaviour by calling him into another room, giving him some kind of enrichment, or invite him into his calm space if you have one set up. Once he has stopped the behaviour and it is safe for you to touch him you can aid the de-escalation process by employing some of the body work, or by putting on a body wrap or Thundershirt.

How to introduce TTouch Bodywork
While doing the TTouches be sure to not lean over your dog, as this might intimidate or frighten him. It is safer for you and more comfortable for your dog if you position yourself to the side of, and just behind his head, so that you are both facing in the same direction. This will enable you to see him and to monitor his responses clearly but without staring directly at him, which he may find confrontational. It also makes it easy for him to move away if he wishes, without having to go through you in order to do so.

Bear in mind that if your dog's stress affects you – which it may do even if you aren't directly aware of it – it can be easy to start doing the TTouches rather fast. This can then have the opposite effect to the one you are trying to produce: generally, doing the TTouches slowly is calming while going faster tends to be stimulating.

Be sensitive to indications from your dog that he has had enough and needs a break. You will find that lots of short sessions often work better than one long one, and can easily be fitted into odd moments during the day when you have a few minutes to spare. It is suggested that the longest you work with your dog should be no more than around twenty minutes, but incorporate a few mini-breaks into the session if needed.

Signs that your dog may need a break include him looking unsettled, moving away from you, becoming distracted, and fidgeting. Stop for a while and allow your dog to reposition himself. If he readily settles down for some more work, continue, but if he responds again in a similar way, then it is probably time to end the session and try again another time.

The TTouches can feel very different to normal petting, so don't be surprised if he appears to struggle with them at first. Very often you will find that you see further improvement after you have finished a session – and what may have been difficult for your dog to cope with today, may be easier for him tomorrow. Give him the benefit of the doubt, keep sessions short and listen to your dog.

Before you start!

Before you get started on using the TTouches, for maximum benefit and to avoid inadvertently stressing your dog or compromising your safety, remember the following golden rules:

If your dog wishes to move away while doing the TTouches, allow him to do so.

Let him choose his position: do not insist that he stands if he feels more comfortable sitting or lying down. Do not physically move your dog around so you can reach parts of his body; you should move around your dog instead.

Practice doing each of the TTouches on your own arms or on a partner or friend's arms or back before trying them on your pet. This will help you to appreciate just how light and subtle you can be. Another human can also give you feedback on how it feels and help you to improve.

Concentrating on what you are doing can sometimes make you stiff and tense, which will make the TTouches feel unpleasant to the recipient. Try to relax and keep your breathing deep and regular. Allowing your dog to hear you breathe deeply and *slowly* will also encourage him to match his rate of breathing to yours, aiding calmness.

Just the weight of your hand is enough to move the skin while performing each of the TTouches, and you can make the contact even lighter still if your dog appears wary of the work. At no time should you press into the body; you are only working with the skin.

Make each of your TTouches as slow as possible.

Constantly observe your dog's body language, as this can indicate his state of mind. You will find Sarah Fisher's book *Unlock Your*

Dog's Potential and Turid Rugaas' book *On Talking Terms with Dogs* helpful; but unless you have a lot of experience in this area it can be easy to misinterpret responses, or miss more subtle ones. You may therefore find it helpful initially to arrange a session with a Tellington TTouch practitioner who can help you develop your powers of observation.

TTouch is something we do ***with*** our animals not ***to*** them. Break it down into smaller steps if needed, or start the work in the Confidence Course (you will find more details about this in the following pages). Better still, contact a guild certified Tellington TTouch practitioner for help if you are having any difficulties in applying the work.

Should your dog show concern about you touching certain parts of his body, return to a place where he is less anxious, and when he relaxes try gradually approaching the difficult area again. If there are other signs such as stiffness, or tautness or changes in temperature of the skin, or changes in the hair colour, direction and texture of the coat, it may indicate the presence of a physical problem; ask your vet to investigate further.

Staying safe

You can do TTouches all over your dog's body, but **observe him closely** as you do so. It cannot be emphasised too often that the most affectionate and placid of dogs can behave unpredictably when stressed, and may strike out unexpectedly if he is frightened or feels unwell or is in pain. If you lack experience in reading canine body language, a Tellington TTouch practitioner will be able to help you in developing this essential skill.

As has already been explained, fear, arousal and

physical conditions are usually evident in your dog's posture as tension patterns. When you gently touch those areas the skin may feel taut and the muscles hard and tight. For a CCD dog this can often be felt in the neck and head, and he may have a very high head carriage. You may even see changes in the coat texture in the neck and down the back, and the tail might be clamped down tightly between the hind legs, or held high and stiff in a state of high arousal. If you can release the tension in these places it can make a big difference, with a more relaxed posture producing a correspondingly calmer and more relaxed state of mind: but using the TTouches to help achieve this needs to be managed with great tact and subtlety as your dog may be particularly sensitive to contact in these areas at first.

Be very gentle and watch him carefully at all times, adapting your actions according to whether they indicate a decreasing or increasing level of concern. You will find reading Turid Rugaas' book *On Talking Terms With Dogs*, and Sarah Fisher's book *Unlock Your Dog's Potential*, which contains detailed information on tension patterns, invaluable guides in helping to develop your observational skills and in interpreting what you see.

You can also try a permissions test to check his concern levels if you are unsure about reading your dog's subtle body language; simply do one or two repetitions of the TTouch you are performing and stop. Take your hands off your dog and move back a little from him. If he re-engages with you by looking in your direction, moving closer, nudging your arm or vocalising by maybe softly whining, whist looking and moving towards you, then continue doing a few more TTouches. Check in often with him though by regularly stopping and asking for permission to continue. If however, your dog moves away when you stop, let him. He may need a drink, or to 'think' about how the work feels. Often they will return and re-engage with you and you can continue but if not, don't force it. Go and do something else instead, play a game, go for a toilet break or finish the session there. Some dogs really do need the work drip fed in micro sessions so be led by your dog and give him the choice.

If he shows a low level of concern, try using a sheepskin mitten, balled up sock or sponge to do the TTouches with. Remember to be very gentle: and in any places where a lot of tension is present, making the skin and muscles very tight, it is especially essential to be light, slow and soft in your movements, so you don't cause discomfort. Doing just one or two TTouches and then pausing can also help the work to be more acceptable.

The TTouches can cause many different sensations through the body, which at first may feel a little weird to your dog. Bear in mind that just because he is tolerating something, it doesn't necessarily mean that he is enjoying it, so act with caution and keep observing his responses closely – although not by staring hard at him, which he may find alarming!

If he is still concerned, or the level of anxiety increases, don't enforce the TTouches. Work instead on a different area which your dog finds easy to cope with; the shoulder perhaps. As he begins to relax a little you may be able to gradually begin to approach and work on the challenging area, very briefly at first, slowly building it up one TTouch at a time. If you are at all unsure, don't persist but seek help from an experienced practitioner.

If your dog has an old injury be particularly careful when approaching the site of it. Even though it may have occurred a long time ago and be completely healed now, he may still be defensive about that part of his body and show anxiety about you touching it, especially when he is stressed. In some cases there may still be residual discomfort in the area, even though to all outward appearances he seems to be fully recovered. He may also have a fear of the memory of pain in that area. If there is any doubt in the matter, ask your vet to check it out.

Remember!
If your dog doesn't like what you're doing, try:
using a lighter pressure:
and/or
a faster or slower speed:
and/or
using a soft-bristled paint brush, sheepskin mitten, sponge or
balled-up sock to introduce the work:
and/or
working on a different part of the body:
and/or
a different TTouch:
and/or
stopping for a short period and letting your dog move around and
think about the experience before trying again:
and/or
making sessions shorter -
some dogs can only cope with a few minutes or a few TTouches at a time to begin with.
Be patient, increasing the number of TTouches and length of each session slowly:

and/or
starting with TTouch ground work and seeking the help of an experienced Tellington TTouch practitioner.

The Tellington TTouches

There are many different TTouches: many of them have been named after the animals that inspired them – this also makes it a fun and easy way of remembering which is which. A few simple and effective ones have been include here that you might like to try, and which can be especially helpful for compulsive behaviour issues. Once you are familiar with them you may like to add others to your repertoire. You can find out more by reading the books recommended in the Further Reading section at the end of this book, or by attending a workshop or demonstration, or working one-to-one with a TTouch practitioner. Details of how to find practitioners are in the Contacts and Resource section. You can also see the TTouches being demonstrated online by visiting You Tube and searching for Tellington TTouch for dogs - you will find plenty of video clips.

Springbok TTouch

The Springbok can be a great TTouch to try if you see your dog starting to go into a cycle or if he is already performing his CCD behaviour. It can often just bring him back into the present, making him more aware of you and what you may be asking him to do instead, such as chewing a treat, or going to his crate to calm down or outside for a play session. Please note, if your dog has aggressive tendencies while carrying out his compulsive behaviour, do not use this TTouch while he is aroused. For these dogs it might be best to start in the ground work, off leash; this can be done either indoors or outside (see the information on ground work further on in this section for details). I would also highly recommend that you work under the guidance of a qualified, experienced TTouch practitioner if you feel your dog shows any signs of aggression.

Visualise the distinctive high jumps of the Springbok antelope as it leaps vertically into the air with all four legs at once, and you'll have a good idea of what this TTouch looks like. It can settle a nervous or hyperactive dog, and if he is so agitated that he cannot listen to you, the Springbok TTouch may be a way in which you can help him come back down to earth and pay attention. Once he starts to settle and focus on you, you can then switch to one of the other TTouches.

1.

Lightly place the tips of the fingers and thumb of one hand on your dog's body, with the thumb about two inches away from your fingers.

Move your fingers and thumb away off the body in a quick, light, upward, sliding motion while simultaneously bringing them together.

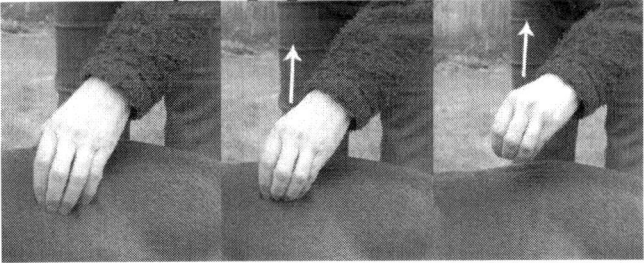

Springbok TTouch   *(photo: Toni Shelbourne)*

2.

For maximum effect this TTouch should be performed randomly and quickly, skipping from one area to another. It can be used on all areas of the body.

Be very careful to keep it feeling light, delicate and airy – do not pinch or pluck at the skin with your fingertips or pull at the coat: take special care if your dog has long hair.

Clouded Leopard & Raccoon TTouches

Because this circular TTouch helps to build trust and improve co-ordination and the ability to learn, it can be really helpful with dogs which are fearful, nervous, stressed and hyperactive. The Clouded Leopard TTouch can be used all over the body, even in areas such as the tail and face. Generally it is easiest to start on your dog's shoulder area and work out from there, returning to this region if need be.

1.
Position yourself to the side and slightly behind your dog. Rest one hand lightly on his body. Softly curve the fingers of your other hand, so that it looks a bit like a leopard's paw. Lightly place the pads of the fingers on your dog's body, with the thumb a little apart from them to help steady your hand. Your wrist should be straight and relaxed at all times to enable the fingers and wrist to rotate as you perform the movement.

2.
Using the pads of the finger tips, gently move your dog's skin in a clockwise circle about 1 cm in diameter. Maintain the same speed for the whole movement.

It helps if you imagine that your fingers are travelling around a clock face: start each circle where the six would be and move in a clockwise direction all the way around the dial – but when you return to the six position again, keep on going to nine o'clock on the clock face so that you have

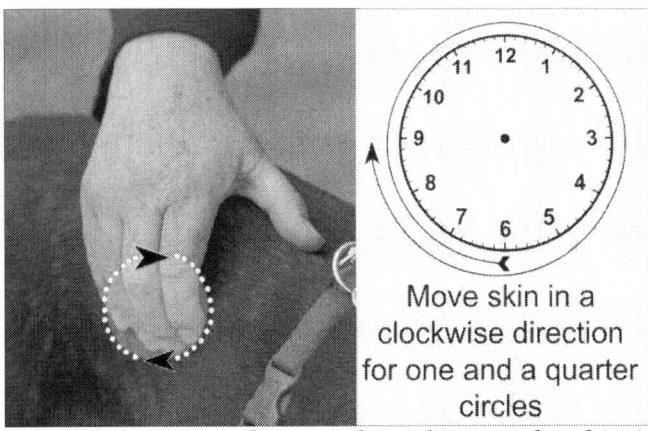

Clouded Leopard TTouch *(photo: Bob Atkins)*

completed one full circle plus a quarter of another one. Try to make your circles as slow as possible.

3.
Keep your wrist and fingers relaxed, and maintain a light but consistent pressure and speed. Do not press into your dog's skin – use no more than just the weight of your hand. After completing each TTouch, stop, and keeping your hand in contact with your dog, pause for a slow breath and then slide your fingers lightly across the coat to a new spot about a hands' width away and begin another circle.

4.
Remember to start each circle at the 'six' point, with six being the point nearest to the ground. Ensure that the skin feels as though you are lightly lifting not dragging it as you start each circle - experiment on your own arm to check.

5.
Remember that you should be moving the skin with your fingers, rather than allowing your fingers to glide over the surface. If your dog is long coated,

you may find it more effective to lightly reposition your fingers into the coat slightly so you can more easily feel his skin.

6.

When working over bony areas, or places where he is concerned about being touched, make your contact with your dog's body much lighter, so you are hardly touching him at all while still moving the skin under your fingers. If the skin feels tight, do not try and force it to move, but try making the circles using a larger surface area (by using either the whole of your hand or half the length of your fingers) and continue to use the lightest of pressures and to be very slow in your movement.

7.

If your dog doesn't like 'connected' TTouches, (i.e. when you link each TTouch by sliding your fingers across the skin from the circle you have just completed to the place where you are going to start the next one, maintaining a constant light contact), try lifting your hand after each circle instead and gently placing it somewhere else on his body. Experiment to see which works best for your dog, and bear in mind that preferences may change from day to day or even hour to hour. Sometimes working randomly over your dog's body can grab the attention of the nervous system better than 'connected' TTouches.

8.

If your dog still appears reluctant about allowing you to work on certain areas of his body, move back to a place where he enjoys the feel of the TTouch and dip in and out of the areas of concern as described previously.

For some dogs, the Clouded Leopard may feel quite intense: if it is too much for him initially try the Llama or Zebra TTouch instead – you can find videos of how to do these on YouTube.

9.
Try changing your hand position slightly to develop into the **Raccoon TTouch** – this is a similar circular movement to the Clouded Leopard but performed using the very tips of the fingers rather than the pads. This makes the movement smaller and more intense. It can be used all over the body and is especially useful when working around small, more sensitive areas such as around the base of the ears or tail, on the face, paws and between the toes.

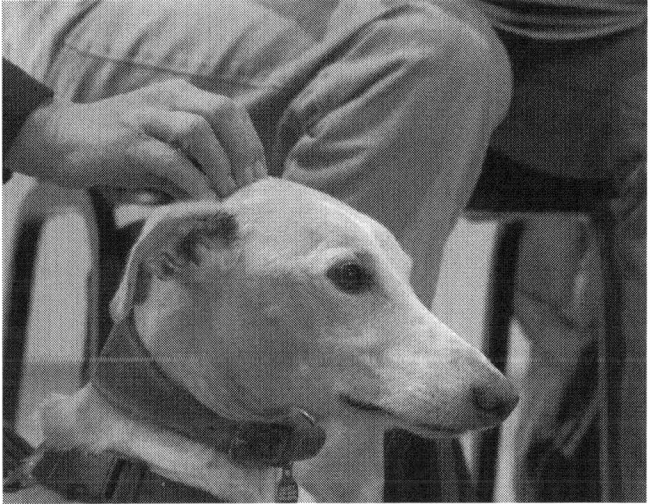

Raccoon TTouch *(photo: Toni Shelbourne)*

Work towards being able to perform Raccoon TTouches all over the muzzle and head. This will help his jaw relax, and aid with issues such as barking, eating inappropriate items, hyperactivity, shadow chasing and fly snapping, etc. Slide your fingers across the skin between each circle for added awareness.

Some dogs may be very sensitive to having the top of the head and face touched, so work slowly, pause often and intersperse with different TTouches in different areas of the body before returning to do a little more work on the neck, head and face.

Alternatively, try introducing touch to your dog's head and face using a soft artist's paint brush, a sheepskin mitten, sponge or even balled-up socks. These items can feel more neutral and will sometimes be more acceptable to your dog than a human hand. Using a brush also enables you to maintain a little distance from your dog, which may help him to tolerate the interaction.

Allow him to investigate the object in your hand first, and then stroke the side of the face along the jaw line, or under the chin first. Use the length, not the tip, of the brush hairs, and once he is relaxed about this, perform some of the circular TTouches, again with the side of the bristles and starting in a less invasive place such as under the chin or on the side of the cheek.

Later you will be able to use your hand on his face and top of the head, but it may take several short sessions spread over a number of days to achieve this. Don't try to rush the process! If the work is especially difficult for him to accept in this area refer to the earlier *Staying Safe* section.

11.

As the face is bony, make your contact as light as possible, so you are hardly touching your dog at all while still gently moving the skin under your fingers. Work towards being able to perform Raccoon TTouches all over the muzzle and head. This will help his jaw relax and aid with all CCD issues.

Use this TTouch to prepare for mouth work, which can be very useful for CCD suffers but may be challenging for some dogs to accept straightaway without some prior preparation.

Coiled Python

The Coiled Python is a combination TTouch where a lift of the skin is incorporated with a circular TTouch such as the Clouded Leopard or Racoon TTouch mentioned above. The circular part of the TTouch heightens the dog's focus and the lift helps him to relax and brings attention to what you are doing. It helps to relax tense areas of skin and muscle, which is particularly relevant for dogs that spin, pounce or hold their head high, as these behaviours exacerbate tension in the neck, shoulders and back. This TTouch can be done with any part of the front of the hand, so the pads, or half the length of the fingers, or the whole hand can be moulded to the body. If an area you are working on feels very tight through the skin and muscle it is recommended that you start with your whole hand in contact with your dog.

1.

With the whole hand moulded to an area of your dog's body, move the skin in a circle and a quarter, just as you do with the Clouded Leopard and Raccoon TTouches (if you have not yet read about or practised the Clouded Leopard yet, return to this section first to learn how to perform a circular TTouch). However, when you reach the nine o'clock position, carry the tissue a little further around the clock face, without pausing, to twelve o'clock, but being careful not to pull the skin.

2.

Once at twelve o'clock pause for a moment before slowly allowing the tissue back around the half circle from twelve o'clock to six o'clock, but this time moving in an anti-clockwise direction from twelve o'clock through nine o'clock and finishing at six o'clock. You will feel the skin wanting to resettle, your job is to support it back down and not drop it into place. If you simply let go of the skin while it is at the twelve o'clock position, it will feel like a sudden lurch to your dog as the skin falls back into place; a most unpleasant sensation.

3.

The slower you can carry and support the tissue back around the half circle from twelve o'clock to the six o'clock position, the more benefit your dog will feel and you should notice a softening of the tension in the area you are working.

4.

Once you have completed the movement, leave your hand in place, pausing for a few seconds before moving to a new area and repeating.

Ear TTouch

Ear work can have a wonderfully calming, comforting and soothing effect, helping to lower stress levels and heart rate when done slowly. The majority of dogs enjoy Ear TTouches, and most owners naturally stroke their dog's ears anyway. Note that for the purposes of TTouch only one ear is stroked at a time, swapping often between the two.

1.

Position yourself so that both you and your dog are facing in the same direction. Lightly place one hand on his body. Use the back of your other hand to stroke softly along the outside of one ear.

2.

If your dog is happy about this, cup your hand around the ear and stroke from the base to the tip. Try to mould as much of your hand as possible around his ear for maximum contact. If your dog has upright ears work in an upwards direction: if they flop downwards, work in a horizontal outwards and downwards direction.

3.
Next, take the ear between the thumb and curved forefingers of one hand so that you only have one layer of ear flap between fingers and thumb. Slide them along the length of the ear, working from the base right out to the end or tip (*below*).

Ear TTouch *(photo: Bob Atkins)*

Move your hand slightly each time you begin a new stroke so that you cover every part of the ear. Be gentle and work slowly to help calm and relax. At the tip of the ear is an acupressure 'shock' point: make a small circle there with the tip of your forefinger to stimulate it, and then slide your fingers off. This is beneficial for dogs that are habitually nervous.

4.
If your dog is holding his ears in a furled, pinned or high ear carriage, very gently unfurl or lower them as you slide along each ear, bringing it into a more natural, relaxed position. Posture can directly affect behaviour, so if the ears are relaxed the rest of the body will tend to follow suit.

5.
The ears of some dogs may have a rather taut connection to the head and can feel very stiff and tight – especially when they are feeling stressed or aroused.

In such instances, try a few small circular Raccoon TTouches (see the section on the Clouded Leopard and Raccoon TTouches above) around the base, or gently move the whole of your dog's ear in a circular motion to help release the tension. The emphasis *must* be on small and subtle movements – while you want to try and relax the ear and surrounding tense area, if you are forcible you may inadvertently cause discomfort.

6.
If your dog appears to dislike ear work and has floppy ears, try moulding your hand over one and gently holding it against his head (*below*).

Ear TTouch *(photo: Sarah Fisher)*

Very slowly and gently move your whole hand in a circular movement, so that his head supports his ear. Make the circle small so that it is a subtle movement; he may prefer it being circled in an anti-clockwise direction to a clockwise one. If he still finds this challenging, try wearing a sheepskin mitten or glove to diffuse the sensation even further.

You may find that this will help to reduce any concerns he has and to become more tolerant about ear work. If he continues to show concern, do ask your vet to check his ears, mouth and neck, as there may be an underlying physical reason for his unease.

Mouth TTouch

Mouth work can be another useful TTouch which can help considerably with CCD behaviours. Working around the face and on the gums can have a positive and beneficial effect on emotional and physical responses, and improves the ability to focus and learn: there is a direct connection between the area at the front of the mouth and the limbic system in the brain, which is the seat of emotional responses and also responsible for functions including adrenaline flow, long term memory and behaviour.

Mouth work is invaluable for dealing with behaviours associated with CCDs or dogs in a state of high arousal. Once accustomed to it you will find he is much more accepting of anything you do around the face and mouth so teeth cleaning and pill giving will be much easier. It is, however, best to use this particular TTouch when you are giving your dog a TTouch session when he is calm. Do not attempt it while he is in the middle of a compulsive cycle: it could be dangerous for you to try at any time when your dog is very stressed - never forget that an aroused dog may behave unpredictably and out of character.

Do not use this TTouch if you think your dog may nip or bite: seek expert help. It is also easier for your dog if you have first worked around the outside of the face, along the jaw and over the whole head with the other TTouches before introducing this one.

1.
Position yourself so that you are to the side of your dog, behind his head and with both of you facing in the same direction. If he turns to face you stop immediately, as this may indicate that he is not comfortable with the work.

2.
Place one hand under his chin for support, but without restricting his movement, while you stroke gently along the sides of his face and muzzle with the back of the other hand.

3.
If he is relaxed about this, use gentle Clouded Leopard or Raccoon TTouches to work around the jaw muscles and lips (*pic A, top right*).

4.
When your dog is comfortable with this, quietly slip a finger or thumb under the lip and up onto the gum. Wet your finger with a little water if the mouth feels dry, so that it slides freely on the gum rather than sticking to it. Gently run the finger around the whole gum line, both upper and lower. Switch hands so you can work the gums on both sides of the mouth (*pic B, bottom right*) You may only be able to do this for very short periods initially. Be prepared to intersperse mouth work with the other TTouches, and keep returning to do a little bit more every so often. If he is very

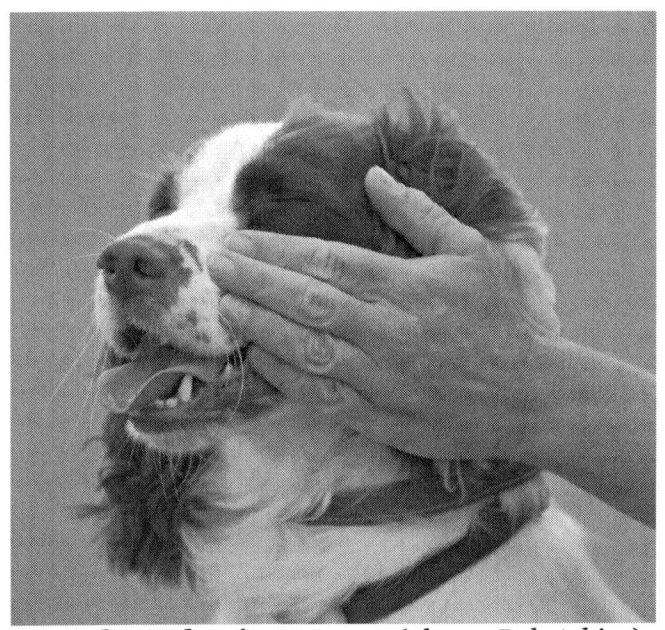

Mouth work: pic A (*photo: Bob Atkins*)

Mouth work: pic B (*photo: Toni Shelbourne*)

uncomfortable with you touching even the outside of his mouth and face you could start the process by stroking along the jaw line with a soft paint brush or doing some of the circular TTouches with a sponge or balled up socks etc. (refer to the *Staying Safe* section).

Tail TTouch

A dog will instinctively stiffen and tuck his tail when frightened, or raise it like a flag if aroused, so helping to release both the physical and emotional tension held there can be key to helping him to cope with his anxieties or behaviours. Although tail work can help to increase confidence in a dog which is nervous, timid and noise sensitive, and calm an overly aroused dog, do not however, assume that he will be happy for you to handle his tail or touch him around his hindquarters. Dogs who are anxious and aroused hold a lot of tension in these areas, so may find it difficult to tolerate contact there and may react defensively. Tail chasers may find it especially difficult. Introduce tail work and working around the hindquarters over a number of sessions, dipping in and out, and interspersing it with other TTouches. If unsure you can always use the permissions test explained earlier to check if he is coping with you working in this area, by doing one or two moments of work in these challenging areas before stopping and watching your dog's reaction.

If in doubt, start to introduce touch to the tail with the Clouded Leopard TTouches or even trying the same circular TTouch motion using the back of your fingers or hand (this is called the Llama TTouch). You can do this while your dog is sitting, so that the floor supports his tail. If he has long hair, you can also try very gently sliding small sections of hair between your fingers from the root to the tip. Do not pull at the hair, but do not be so light that you produce a tickly sensation, and keep your movements slow and smooth.

As with mouth work, this TTouch may be too difficult for your dog to cope with when he is aroused, but ensure you have done plenty in your regular sessions when he is calm. The tail should go from feeling very stiff to being loose and flexible.

1.
While your dog is standing or lying down on his side, with one hand gently take hold of the tail at its base, near his bottom. Lightly support it from underneath with your fingers, and with your thumb lying on top, the tip of which faces towards your dog's head (*pic A below*). Lightly place your other hand on your dog's hindquarters or under the thigh.

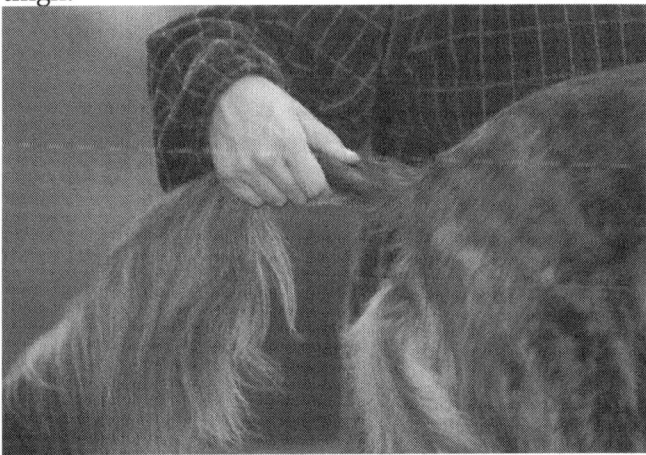

Tail work TTouch: pic A　　*(photo: Bob Atkins)*

2.
Move the tail slowly and gently in both clockwise and then anti-clockwise directions, making sure that you keep within a comfortable range of

movement. These movements need to be tiny and it can be very easy to over-exaggerate them, so it is a good idea to practise on your own fingers first to see just how little movement is needed to create an effect, and then to apply the same gentle and subtle rotation to your dog's tail. At first the tail may feel rather wooden and hard to move; work on it for very short periods if your dog shows reluctance for you to touch him in this area, and be very tactful and gentle. After a while you should notice that the range of movement gradually increases and that your dog becomes happier to have you perform this TTouch. This can take time and several sessions for some dogs.

3.
If your dog is very nervous, or clamps his tail down, don't try and pull it out but instead cup the palm of your hand over the top of his tail where it joins his body and gently make small clockwise and anti-clockwise circular movements (*pic B below*).

From this you can progress to gently holding your dog's tail against one of his own hind legs and then,

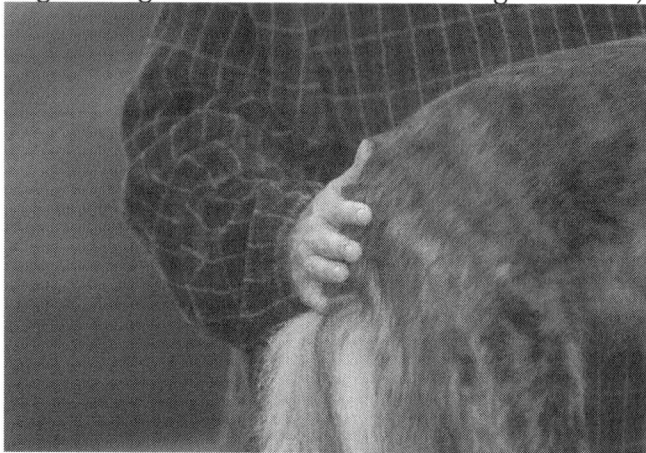

Tail work TTouch: pic B   (*photo: Bob Atkins*)

starting from the base, using the whole of your hand to do circular TTouches along its length all the way down to the tip. Complete each circle with a pause before sliding a little further down the tail and repeating. Fit in as many circles as you can.

4.
As well as circling the tail, you can also perform a 'pearling' action along the whole length of the tail: slide your hand along the tail, from base to tip, with your fingers in the same position as in step 1. Each time you feel a vertebra, gently rock it in a downward and inwards movement towards the dog's body. This must be done very, very gently, without exaggerating the movement and while paying very close attention to your dog's responses. Again, you can practise this on your own finger before trying it on your dog.

5.
No tail? No problem – even if your dog's tail is docked, you can still gently work the stump using the circular rotations or by doing Raccoon TTouches along its length (*pic C below*).

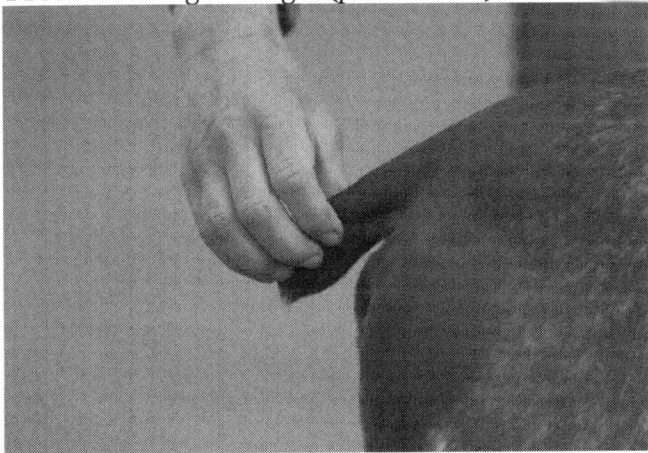

TTouch Tail work: pic C　　*(pic:Bob Atkins)*

Tellington TTouch Body wraps

In addition to the special TTouches, the Tellington TTouch system makes use of many different training aids, one of the most recognizable being body wraps. They can be very successful with dogs that suffer from CCDs, as well as with issues that may be aggravating the behaviour, such as noise sensitivity, stress and other anxieties.

Employing stretchy bandages, they influence the tactile part of the sensory system and the constant gentle pressure can have a very positive calming effect on the nervous system, often quietening or stopping CCD behaviours. Wearing one regularly may result in the frequency of episodes diminishing, the intensity of the action reducing, or you may be able to distract your dog more quickly and divert him to more appropriate activities

The body wrap is also brilliant at bringing awareness of movement to the wearer; often stereotypical CCD movements like spinning will lessen as the dog becomes aware that he is performing the action; the act may have become so habitual, he may have little idea he is actually repeating it. Once you know what you are doing, you have the ability to change it, and that is precisely what the body wrap can achieve: a new-found state of awareness.

It is important that the bandage you use is stretchy, as this allows it to exert a light pressure which stays in constant contact with your dog's body as he moves, without restricting his movement. ACE wraps are ideal and come in a range of lengths and widths according to the size of your dog: if you have difficulty getting hold of them, they can be purchased from the UK Tellington TTouch Guild Office shop (see the Contacts & Resources section at the end). Alternatives include equine tail or exercise bandages sold in equestrian stores, or a crepe bandage if you can't get hold of anything else. Do not use Vetrap or other cohesive bandages, as it is hard to undo quickly if necessary, and the hairs of long-coated dogs can get caught up in it. Make sure there is plenty of give in the fabric of the bandage you use; with time and use the stretchiness eventually becomes lost and the wrap

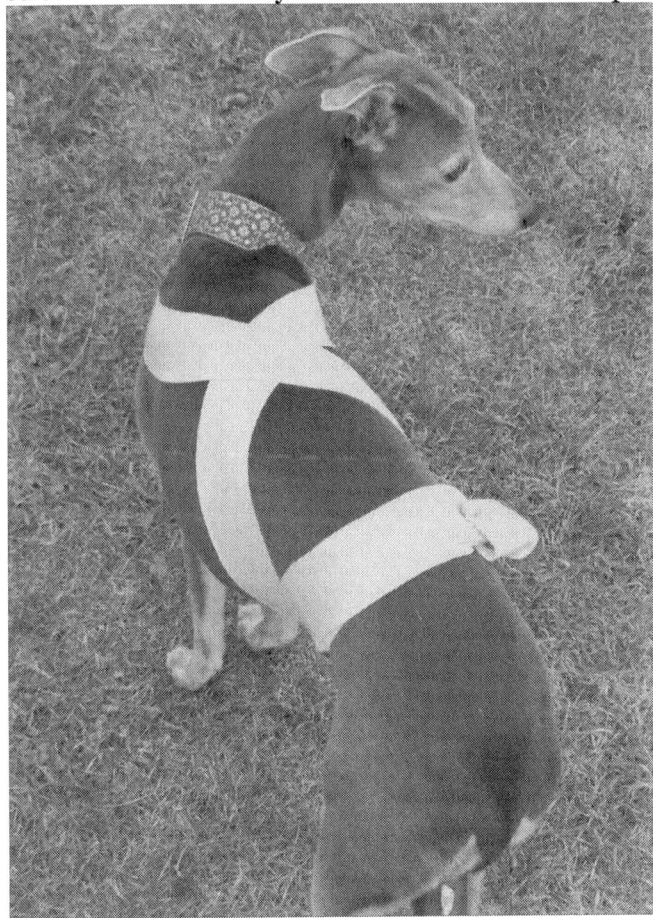

TTouch Half Wrap *(pic: Toni Shelbourne)*

will need replacing.

Introduce the wrap in familiar surroundings where your dog feels safe and is relaxed. Only when he is completely accustomed to, and comfortable wearing it should you use it on him while he is stressed and more likely to get into a cycle of compulsive behaviour.

If you find that a wrap doesn't seem to help much on the first occasion that you use it, do persevere, and try using it in conjunction with the TTouches and ground work. Even if you find that a wrap or Thundershirt (see following section) used by itself helps a lot, it is still worthwhile also doing some TTouches, as this often enhances the effect even further, helping your dog to make positive, permanent changes. Both TTouches and Body Wraps have a cumulative effect, so use them regularly; I would suggest daily for a CCD dog.

Once familiar with the wrap, if you know your dog's triggers for the compulsive behaviour, try putting the body wrap on just before he is likely to start, and see if it helps him calm down and if it is easier for you to divert him on to other activities. If he has already commenced the behaviour, and only if it is safe to do so, and he is comfortable and used to the wrap, put it on him and watch to see if the behaviour starts to de-escalate.

The Half Wrap

Body wraps can be used in a variety of different configurations to help in resolving a wide number of issues, but initially you should start with a simple half wrap - you may find that for many dogs this is quite sufficient, anyway. Provided you introduce it properly, most dogs enjoy wearing a wrap, but even if you think your pet looks a bit comical in it, don't laugh at him - dogs can be just as sensitive as people about being ridiculed.

1.

Approach your dog calmly with the wrap, and with it bundled up in your hand, let him sniff at, and take a good look at it. Do not rush this stage. Stroke it gently against his sides and chest. You can even use it to do some circular TTouches on his shoulders and chest. If he is anxious about approaching it, place the wrap on the floor and put treats on top of it for him to eat.

2.

Once your dog is quite happy around the wrap, unroll and pass the centre of the bandage around the front of his chest. Bring the ends up across the shoulders, up over his back and cross them over just above his shoulder blades (*below*).

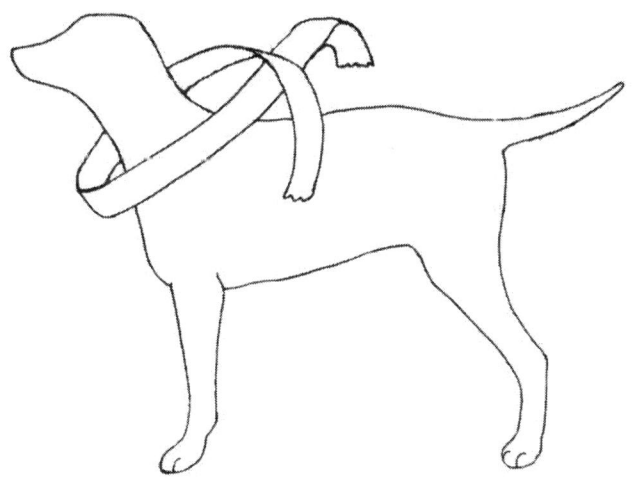

3.

Take both loose ends down the sides of his ribcage, behind the front legs. Cross them beneath his rib cage and bring them back up again over the top of his back. As you do this, keep the wrap close to his body and unravel it a little at a time from your hands so it doesn't flap around (*below*). Be careful not to inadvertently pull the ends too much at this stage, as some dogs may find this difficult to cope with. Try to be slow and smooth in your movements.

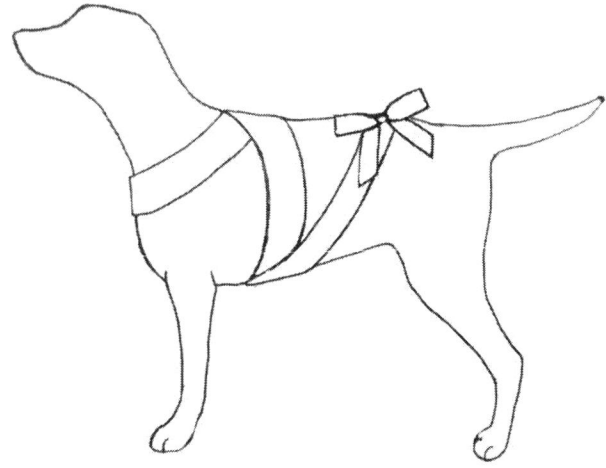

4.
Tie the ends in a bow or quick release knot so it can be quickly undone again if necessary. Make sure that the fastening lies off to one side of the spine, not directly on top of it. Alternatively, sew some Velcro to the bandage ends to secure it.

The wrap should be applied just firmly enough to keep it in place and enable it to maintain contact with the body – about the same sort of pressure as an elasticated tracksuit waistband. Check in various places to see if you can easily slide your hand beneath it. If it is too tight in one area and too loose in another, readjust it until the tension is the same throughout. Remember that its purpose is to provide feelings of security and sensory input, not to support, and it certainly shouldn't restrict movement or cause discomfort.

5.
Encourage your dog to move while wearing the wrap: if he freezes, use gentle coaxing, offer a really tasty treat or invite a gentle game with a favourite toy to overcome his reluctance. If he rubs or grabs at it, try to distract him. If after a few minutes he is still worrying at it or not moving, remove it and try again on another day. Before applying the wrap again, do more TTouches on him by way of preparation for wearing it.

6.
Even if your dog seems comfortable the first time he wears a wrap, remove it after a few minutes, and over the next few sessions gradually increase the duration it is worn for. Do not rush this process or be tempted to put it on before he is comfortable if performing a CCD behaviour.

Never leave your dog alone while he is wearing a wrap in case he gets caught up. Keep a close eye on him in case you need to make adjustments for comfort or safety, or if he wants it taken off. On very rare occasions some dogs appear to not tolerate body wraps at all. This may be down to an underlying health or pain issue so do consult your vet.

You can find out more about using body wraps in 'All Wrapped Up For Pets: Improving function, performance and behaviour with Tellington TTouch Body Wraps' by Robyn Hood (see Further Reading).

Thundershirt
In recent years various products have appeared on the market which can be used as an alternative to a

body wrap. The best known of these is probably the Thundershirt, produced by a company which worked alongside Linda Tellington Jones in its development. The Thundershirt's comfortable, constant contact has a similar calming effect to a wrap, is easy to put on, and adjusts to fit different body shapes. If your dog tends to move around a lot when he is in a cycle of behaviour the Thundershirt may stay on better than the bandage, but it can be harder to put on so you will need to weigh up the pros and cons of each and go for what will work best for you and your dog. Both can be very effective.

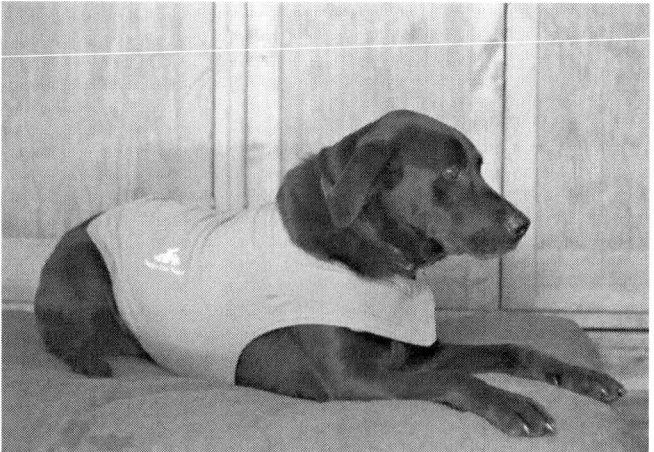

Thundershirt *(photo: Sarah Fisher)*

As when using wraps, a Thundershirt should be introduced carefully, breaking the process down into easy stages. It is secured using Velcro straps, and before fitting it, you should make sure that your dog is comfortable with the sound they make. Extra training and time may be required for dogs with hyper-noise sensitivity. Spend some time over a few sessions introducing the noise to him, but if the sound of the Velcro is just too much for him, I'd suggest that you stick with a body wrap or try using a close-fitting doggie T-shirt instead.

The first step in introducing the Thundershirt is to allow your dog to inspect it. Putting it on the floor and placing a few really tasty treats on top will encourage him to check it out and help in creating a positive association and overcoming any concerns he may have about it. Next, unfold it half way and lay it across his back for a few moments, offering a few more treats if necessary, as he gets used to the feeling.

If he is fine with this, open the Thundershirt up completely and put it on, closing the front fastening but leaving the side panels open. When your dog is happy about this, close the side panels to create a snug fit. As with using wraps, keep the initial introductory sessions and periods wearing it short; but once your dog is accustomed to wearing it, it can be left on for as long as required (weather permitting) although you should not leave him in it unsupervised.

Tellington TTouch Groundwork: The Confidence Course

Known as the Confidence Course or playground of higher learning, what at first glance may look like an obstacle course is far from it. As the name suggests, the object of the exercise is to promote confidence rather than to intentionally trip up, confuse or impede your dog. It encourages clear, rational thinking and planning – things that often go out the window when fear or over arousal is present – and as your dog makes his way around it, can help him to make massive shifts for the better in his thinking and responses. As well as boosting confidence, this exercise is also terrific for developing cooperation, coordination and communication between you. It is also very mentally tiring so can be excellent, appropriate, stimulation for CCD dogs.

While groundwork is suggested here as a way of helping your dog to cope with his CCD, you may find that it can benefit him in other areas too. Because it improves proprioception it is very useful in teaching agility dogs to move more effortlessly and efficiently, or to help dogs that pull on the leash to find their balance. It can similarly be used for older dogs as a low impact exercise to maintain flexibility and provide mental stimulation.

You can set up a Confidence Course outdoors or indoors – working inside can give your dog something else to do and think about instead of his compulsion, especially if that is generally where he performs these actions. You should, however, have already introduced your dog to the idea in advance so that it is something which he is by now familiar with.

You do not need lots of expensive equipment, but can easily improvise using objects you either already have to hand or can buy very cheaply.

Short lengths of plastic guttering, plastic

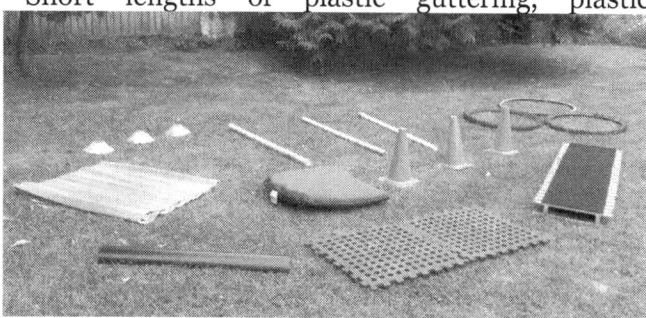

Everyday items for a Confidence Course – spread them well apart before taking your dog around them. *(photo: Toni Shelbourne)*

plumbing pipes, foam pipe lagging or old broom handles make great poles which can be laid out on the ground for your dog to walk over. Slightly raise one or both ends of some poles by crushing an empty drink can in the centre to form a rest for the pole; or scatter them in a random 'pick up sticks' style pile which he has to pick his way through.

Use old bicycle tyres or children's hula hoops to similarly create mini-mazes to walk through. A short length of scaffold plank can be stepped over or walked along: raise one or both ends by placing a piece of half-profile plastic guttering beneath to create a low raised walkway. Use pieces of carpet, rubber bath mats, non-slip plastic and other materials to provide different textures and feels beneath his paws - you could even press the doormat from the front door into service! If you have a foam mattress from a garden lounger it will create a surface that yields slightly as he walks across it, giving yet another different experience: indoors you could use cushions from the sofa or pillows from your bed.

Try introducing a slalom, setting out a line of plastic squash bottles weighted by half filling them with water, or empty upturned plastic plant pots, or sports cones which he can weave in and out of. Be inventive and imaginative – as long as the objects you choose are safe, you can create endless variations to keep your dog engaged.

Once you have a few obstacles set up, pop your dog on the leash so you can help to guide him to each one in turn and can encourage him to slow down if he tries to rush. It is best to use a harness rather than attaching the leash to the collar, as an inadvertent tug on his neck which raises his head can put him into a state of arousal, which is exactly the opposite effect to the one you are trying to create.

Ask your dog to approach and then slowly move over, through or onto each of the obstacles in turn – it is not a race! If he rushes, he is more likely to become unbalanced and to make mistakes. Moving slowly will encourage him to move with greater deliberation and precision, developing his physical control and self-restraint. Vary the routes you take around the Confidence Course and the order and direction in which you approach each obstacle. Ask him to stop frequently, both in front of and after completing each obstacle, as well as while standing on it so he can collect himself physically, mentally and emotionally. Halting will help make him more aware of his movements, and encourage him to focus his attention on the task in hand and to carefully plan his next move.

If you need to give a light signal on the leash to encourage your dog to slow down or stop, remember to gently and slowly allow the tension on it to go slack afterwards, otherwise you will interfere with his balance.

Once he is focused on the ground work exercises, you can carefully introduce perceived threats or triggers such as other dogs or people, or teach self-control around high arousal situations like cyclists and joggers: or in this case, give him an alternative to performing his compulsive behaviour. With another focus, i.e. concentrating on working round the Confidence Course, the behaviour can become more measured at first and over time diminish, and with the aid of reward-based training and the other TTouch tools, a dog can learn to be calm in these highly charged periods. As already mentioned, ground work can help a dog to make massive changes in the way he responds to situations, helping to guide him into making a more measured response instead of flipping into an aroused state and going into a cycle of inappropriate behaviour.

For dogs who aren't comfortable on a leash or inclined to be grabby or aggressive when hyper, you can do the ground work off leash instead. Use some very high value treats to encourage him to investigate the obstacles, and set up a few mats as stations where you ask him to sit or do a down and wait for a few seconds before moving on to the next obstacle. Remember, you are aiming for him to walk on, over and through them slowly and calmly, so take your time encouraging concentration and accuracy through the course.

You can see the Confidence Course being demonstrated online: visit You Tube and search for 'Tellington TTouch for Dogs' and you will find plenty of video clips.

Seeking help from a certified TTouch practitioner

There are many more tools that a TTouch practitioner can show you which may benefit your dog; some of these need to be supervised or first introduced by an experienced person. If you find the above techniques seem to help but you need more guidance, please don't hesitate to ask for professional help.

Other useful Holistic options
There are various other modalities that may be useful for CCD suffers. If used together with the TTouch method and other advice in this book, they can be an important piece in the jigsaw puzzle to recovery. While TTouch blends well and safely with all other holistic methods or conventional medication, this may not be true of others; be aware that essential oils and homeopathy don't mix well together, for example, as the oils may cancel out the homeopathic affects.

With any therapy or product, bear in mind that just because it is described as being 'natural' or is safe for you to use, it doesn't automatically mean it is safe for your dog. Some can interfere with medication, or shouldn't be given where certain health issues are present, or to young puppies or pregnant dogs. Trained professionals in all the fields mentioned below should be consulted, both for the safety of your dog and to achieve the greatest measure of success.

Bach remedies
In common with other holistic modalities, Bach Flower Essences (not to be confused with aromatic floral sprays) can be helpful with a wide variety of emotional issues which may contribute to compulsive behaviours. They are not sedatives or tranquilizers, but act to gently address and rebalance emotions and mental states of mind, which makes them particularly appropriate with dogs who are reactive and obsessive. They can be used in conjunction with conventional as well as homeopathic and herbal remedies, and can provide support when working through the TTouch training and other suggestions in this book. They are very safe to use - as far as I am aware, adverse effects

have never been reported; but I would suggest that, as always, you err on the side of safety and check first with your vet before giving them to your pet.

You may find that Bach Flower Essences can benefit you as well as your dog - if you tend to become stressed by your dog's behaviour, your emotional output can cause him to become anxious or exacerbate any worries he already has.

Bach Flower Essences can be bought over the counter at most high street chemists and health shops as well as online. Pet-friendly alcohol-free versions are now available, although normal ones are fine to use and if diluted, your dog may object less to the taste of the brandy the remedies are preserved in.

Bach Rescue Remedy is probably the best known of all the essences, and can help take the edge off your dog's anxiety. Useful in emergency situations or at times of stress, it is a combination of five different flower essences: Star of Bethlehem (shock and trauma), Rock Rose (terror), Clematis (faintness), Impatiens (agitation), and Cherry Plum (loss of control), and is useful for general calming. The Impatiens and Cherry Plum included in the remedy may be useful when your dog is in the grip of his compulsion, and you could safely spray some into the room he is in to see if it helps; see instructions on administration below. It may not be precisely the right combination for your dog, but can be the remedy you reach for to give you breathing space while considering which of the more specific remedies are indicated. It can't hurt but it might help.

You might like to research other flower essences, which will more specifically address your dog's issues: choose the remedy or remedies you feel best fit your dog's anxieties. Don't worry if you choose the 'wrong' one: if it isn't right for your dog it will simply have no effect, and no harm will come of it. Flower essences which may have particular relevance include:

White Chestnut: The remedy for unwanted thoughts and mental arguments, which go around and around your head repetitively. White Chestnut is said to calm these thoughts and help us to think straight.

Crab Apple: I suggest you mix this with the White Chestnut, as it is THE remedy for obsessive behaviours.

Olive: The remedy for exhaustion. If your dog physically and mentally wears himself out with his compulsive action, then Olive may be useful.

Oak: Likewise, if he struggles on with his CCD regardless of injury, illness or exhaustion, Oak may be needed to help him stop.

A single remedy may be sufficient and work very effectively; but where there are several issues, you can combine several essences (up to six or eight) to make up your own mix specifically tailored to your dog. As with homeopathy, the better the match to the individual, the more successful the outcome is likely to be.

You may see very rapid results if the correct remedies have been selected, sometimes within minutes, but it can take longer, so persevere for at least two and preferably three to four weeks. Perversely, the milder the problem is, the longer it can take to see beneficial results; and bear in mind that irregular and missed doses may cause the remedies to be less effective.

Administration

If you want to give multiple remedies it is easiest if you make up a remedy bottle. Take a small clean bottle or jar (small bottles with a dropper top can be bought inexpensively from the chemist). Fill with fresh clean water – bottled mineral water for preference – and add to this two drops of each remedy (up to six or eight different flower essences) you have chosen. Put the cap or lid on, shake to mix it and store it in the fridge. Discard anything that is left over after a week and make up a fresh batch.

Give four drops of the remedy you have selected as being most appropriate for your dog, or from the remedy bottle you have made up, four times daily. If you miss a dose or struggle to give the doses spaced apart you can either:

- Give first thing in the morning and last thing at night as well as in his feeds.
- If you know he drinks regularly through the day, you can put eight drops in his water bowl so he regularly gets doses throughout the day - it doesn't matter how much you dilute the remedy for it still to be effective. Check though that he is still happy to drink from a bowl with the remedies in as he may be able to detect the difference. If you are worried place two bowls down, one with the remedy and one with plain water.
- You can give the doses close together, so if you miss a dose, give another a couple of hours later.
- Take a clean spray bottle, fill with mineral water and add up to ten drops, and when he needs an extra dose, spray it into the room he is in.

Don't worry if you accidentally give too many or too few drops – overdosing is virtually impossible, and it is more important that you dose regularly each and every day. In fact, if he is having a bad day, you can dose more frequently to aid him to settle quicker.

Safety and tips on administration

Bach Flower Essences can be administered in various ways. Never try to give them directly into your dog's mouth from the glass dropper just in case he bites it. Instead, put a few drops on your fingers which your dog can lick off, or add them to a water bowl or food, or offer on small pieces of dry bread or treats which will absorb the liquid. Bear in mind that if your dog is feeling stressed or won't eat at the time, the remedies can also be dropped onto the top of the nose or wiped along the lips where he will reflexively lick them off. Alternatively, they can be applied to the pads of the paws, on the belly, or to the acupoint which lies halfway between his ears by dropping the remedy onto the palm of your hand and then stroking it onto the top of his head. If administered externally in this way, dose as frequently as you would if giving them orally. Choose whichever method causes the least stress to your dog, and is easy and safe for you to do.

You can find out more about Bach Flower remedies from The Bach Centre (details can be found in the Contacts and Resource Section).

Homeopathy

Homeopathy addresses the whole body, so can be effective in resolving emotional issues as well as physical problems. Pioneered and developed by Samuel Hahnemann in the eighteenth century, it is based on the principle that 'like cures like' following his discovery that substances which produced the same symptoms as an ailment, could, when given in much smaller quantities, cure it. These substances are diluted in a special process known as potentisation, and subjected to succussion (vigorous shaking) which increases the homeopathic strength even though the chemical concentration decreases.

Homeopathy is a very safe modality, and if the wrong remedy is chosen, it will simply have no effect and do no harm. Homeopathic remedies are obtainable from chemists, health shops and online, where they are most commonly supplied as 6c or 30c 'potencies'. This refers to the dilution and succussion of the remedy – the higher the number the more times it has undergone this process and the more powerful the effect may be.

The success of homeopathy relies on closely matching the right remedy (or remedies) to the individual, taking into account not only physical symptoms but background, lifestyle, environment, demeanour, character, likes, dislikes, fears, diet, household and family details, and responses to various external influences. As the remedy for your dog may be very different from the remedy for someone else's dog with the same behaviours, I recommend that you seek professional help - bear in mind that very often the symptoms can be a manifestation of deeper fears and as such are best dealt with by a homeopathic veterinary practitioner.

Homeopathic remedies come in liquid, pill or crystal form and need to be stored and administered correctly: the general advice is that they should not be given with food, or close to mealtimes, and should be stored away from strong smells and direct sunlight. Avoid handling them as this can also destroy their efficacy. Keep them in their original container, and if you drop a pill on the floor, discard it.

As they aren't unpleasant tasting there isn't usually a problem with giving them, although you can if necessary crush pills between two spoons into a fold of paper and tip them into your dog's mouth so they stick to his tongue. The liquid remedies can sometimes be easier to manage - you will know your dog and which form will be the simplest to give.

Allow fifteen minutes before or after eating, and at least five minutes between remedies if you are giving more than one. Simply tip into the bottle cap if giving pills or crystals (some bottles have a handy dispenser system that releases single pills into the cap), open your dog's mouth, and tip in. Do not let the cap come into contact with your dog's mouth. If you do find any difficulties in dosing, try adding ten drops of a liquid remedy to his water bowl - but remember just how acute a dog's senses are, and check that he continues to happily drink from that bowl. As with the Bach Flower Remedies, I recommend you give him choice by putting down two bowls, one with the remedy and one without.

If you would like to find out more about homeopathy or to contact a homeopathic veterinary practitioner, details can be found in the Further Reading and the Contacts & resources section.

Applied Zoopharmacognosy

Essential oils and floral sprays (plant essences in a more diluted form, and also called aromatic waters – not to be confused with Bach and other flower essences), can be another powerful and effective way of helping your dog if he suffers from CCD.

Applied Zoopharmacognosy is not quite the same as aromatherapy, which you may be familiar with in a human context: an AZ practitioner is more akin to an herbalist who possesses an in-depth knowledge of pharmacokinetics than to an Aromatherapist. The essential oils are used differently with animals, employing a process of 'self-selection' whereby the most suitable oil or oils are selected by allowing your dog to do the actual choosing himself. This is done by offering him in turn those which you think are likely to be the most helpful. This is done slowly, with the open bottle held approximately 30 cm to one metre away from his nose, and his reaction to each carefully observed. It is crucial that only high quality oils, prepared especially for this purpose are used - those intended for use in burners are not suitable.

Oils should never be forced on your dog with burners and diffusers, or applied to his body, unless he clearly indicates that he wants this. If you wish to use a burner or diffuser in your home for your own benefit, then do leave a door open so that your dog can move to another room if he wishes.

Offering oils

Before offering any oils to your dog, you should take the time to create a good working environment. In a multi-pet household, other animals should be shut away while working with the oils; but your dog should have the option available at all times of leaving the room you are working in. Prop the door open and leave him off the leash so he is always free to move away if he wishes. It is also nice to have a comfortable dog bed in the room so that if he wants to, he can lie down while working with the oils; and ensure that a bowl of drinking water is available. Oils should be offered at a time when your dog has few distractions; not, for example, near to the time when he is usually fed or when he is anticipating going for a walk. Plenty of time should be set aside, as some dogs may want to work with the oils for an extended period, especially the first time they are offered.

Different dogs may choose different oils for a

similar issue; some may choose more than one, and they may also need the oils to be offered in a specific order, so finding the right oils can be a very individual matter. Upon being offered the oils, your dog's responses need to be carefully noted and correctly interpreted.

The process of narrowing down and then fine-tuning the most appropriate oil or oils is not always a simple procedure. Knowledge of the actions of the oils is essential: they can be *very* potent, and some may not be appropriate to use where certain health conditions are present or if your dog is pregnant or receiving certain medication. They may also lessen or extinguish completely the effect of any homeopathic remedies that are being given.

If you wish to explore this fascinating modality, I suggest that you first read Caroline Ingraham's informative book *Help Your Dog Heal Itself,* which explains the whole process in more detail than there is room for here, together with details of a number of oils. Alternatively, you could arrange a consultation with an AZ practitioner, who will have a wide range of oils which your dog can select from. Do check that the practitioner is up-to-date in their knowledge; a register is currently being compiled – see the Contacts and Resources section for further details.

One final note: what your dog needs may not be what *you* need. You may have adverse reactions to certain oils, such as disliking the smell, or finding that it makes you feel sleepy, unwell or it reacts with medication you are on. It is best to be cautious so do consult the practitioner you are working with in order to be on the safe side.

Pet Remedy

A product called Pet Remedy has recently become

widely available in pet shops and online, bought as either a spray, diffuser or battery operated atomiser; many owners have reported good effects in a variety of stressful situations. The manufacturer's information states that it is a low dosage Valerian blend (it also contains Vetiver, Sweet Basil and Sage) but because it is based on essential oils, I would suggest that you observe the same guidelines as for Applied Zoopharmacognosy: first see if your dog likes the smell, by offering him the option of sniffing at the spray applied to your hand or a tissue, or if using the diffuser, leaving a door open so that he can either stay or leave the room if he wishes. The spray is handy to give an emergency dose if your dog is anxious (sprayed into the room or on a tissue for him to sniff, not directly on your dog), but I suggest that for the maximum effect, you try the diffuser plugged into the room he spends the most time in.

Adaptil
Adaptil (previously known as DAP) is a synthetic copy of a natural canine pheromone produced by nursing bitches, which helps to comfort and reassure their puppies. It can also help adult dogs, promoting calmness and reducing anxiety during times of stress. It is colourless and odourless, with no sedative effect, and can be safely used alongside medications to help your dog feel safe and secure.

It is available from vets, pet shops and online in the form of impregnated collars, reusable diffusers (similar to air freshener devices), and as a spray. The diffuser is plugged into an electrical socket and left continuously running in the room in your house where your dog spends the majority of his time. It covers up to 50-70 square metres, and will last for around 4 weeks; refill vials can be bought and replaced as needed. The positive effect of the diffuser can also be further supported by applying the Adaptil spray to the room your dog is performing his behaviour, if he needs some extra support and is away from the plug-in.

If your dog uses many rooms, or the behaviour occurs outside, you may want to consider using the collar, but beware of the safety issues of leaving a dog or multiple dogs unattended with collars on.

Adaptil also produce non-pheromone based tablets which may be effective for some dogs.

Herbal Remedies and Nutritional Supplements

Herbalism is one of the most ancient forms of medicine. Nowadays you will find plenty of commercial herbal preparations available through vets, online, and stocked in pet stores, which claim to relieve or reduce general anxiety. Herbal remedies should, however, always be treated with great respect and used with care; I suggest that for your pet's welfare you always err on the side of caution and consult a vet knowledgeable in the use of herbs. Always bear in mind that just because a product is advertised as being 'natural' or 'traditional' it doesn't mean that it is either safe or suitable for your dog. Many - including some well-known commercial preparations - have no research to support their claims of efficacy. Some may be harmful to use where certain health issues are present, and they should never be given alongside conventional drugs except under the advice of a veterinary surgeon with appropriate knowledge and experience in this area, in case they conflict with the medication or even combine with it to produce toxic doses. Care should also be exercised in using herbal preparations in conjunction with homeopathy or Applied Zoopharmacognosy.

Do not give your dog herbal preparations formulated for humans except under veterinary advice, as what is good for people isn't always good for dogs. Even where a product is labelled as being specifically for dogs, do still check and research all the ingredients and, once again, consult with a vet if you have any concerns. Many of the 'calming' herbal remedies contain ingredients including skullcap, valerian, passionflower, marshmallow, chamomile, lemon balm, vervain, and lime flowers, all of which are commonly considered as being relatively safe in small doses – but some also contain hops, the flower cones of which are generally regarded as being toxic to dogs. Even those herbs deemed to be 'relatively safe' are not necessarily appropriate for all dogs: valerian for example, may be unsuitable for dogs who are pregnant or suffering from liver disease, and shouldn't be given prior to surgical procedures requiring anaesthesia. Dosage guidelines should be very carefully followed – more is not better, and can often be harmful if given in excess; there may also be cumulative effects with some herbs, making them unsuitable for long term use.

How they are said to work
Some of the active ingredients in commercial herbal products are said to influence Gamma Amino Butyric Acid (GAGA): this is an inhibitory neurotransmitter that works alongside glutamate, which is the main neurotransmitter that fires up arousal, anxiety, memory formation, muscle tension, and the process that leads to the brain developing epilepsy or seizures, which is known as epileptogenesis. Giving a supplement that increases GAGA should then, in theory reduce the symptoms produced by glutamate. Others work to increase

serotonin, which influences mood, impulsivity, social behaviour, digestion, sleep patterns, and so on. The problem is that everything works in conjunction and in fine balance with each other: therefore by altering one, are we incorrectly affecting another? You might prefer to simply give your dog the ability to maintain these primary functions himself by providing him with the building blocks for good health. This includes reducing stress, no or limited use of chemicals, and of course, providing a good species-appropriate diet.

Although an appropriate, carefully selected herbal, homeopathic, flower or essential oil remedy may help in taking the edge off stress levels if your dog is anxious, it is unlikely that, used on their own, they will prove to be a miracle cure for your dog's CCD issues. It may, however, be beneficial when used to provide support to changes to his management, mental stimulation, and to aid training programmes such as the Tellington TTouch Method. Do observe your dog very carefully when using any of these modalities and if you feel they are not having the desired effect, or are even causing an adverse effect, stop giving them immediately and consult your vet or holistic canine qualified practitioner.

Diet
Diet can hugely affect our mood, health and behaviour. With the growth of commercial, cheap pet foods, dogs are increasingly being fed inappropriate constituents such as cereal and meat derivatives. We know from chapter two that many dogs with obsessive licking behaviours are suffering from an imbalance in the gut. We also know that

behaviours such as hyperactivity can greatly improve through a change in diet. Think very carefully about what goes in your dog's bowl; read the ingredients on the packaging and ask yourself if you know what all the ingredient are, and would you be happy to eat this food day in, day out?

Do some research and talk to canine nutritional experts ... Yes, they do exist! You might like to join the Facebook page Holistic Dog Care where you will find not only professional nutritional help but advice from many experienced dog owners. I have suggested a few websites, books and contacts in the Further Reading and the Contacts and Resources sections to help you get started.

Some dogs with digestive problems improve greatly when their gut is supported, with CCD type behaviours disappearing, only to re-emerge if the gut goes out of balance again. Owners report that their IBS suffering dog improves when they have a Vitamin B injection, or that once the acid reflux is treated the fly snapping or licking improves - so don't rule out gut issues as a cause.

Drugs

As mentioned in the first chapters your vet should always be your first port of call when you start to work with your CCD dog. If there is an underlying cause, this must be addressed; it is then your choice whether you do this conventionally or holistically, or with a combination of both.

If you choose to go down the conventional drug route (which if you follow the suggestions in this book, hopefully you won't need to, unless your dog is having seizures or has a true abnormality of the brain), your veterinary surgeon may prescribe a suitable pharmaceutical. It should always be used in conjunction with a behaviour programme, as studies show that although some drugs can help diminish the CCD behaviour, it is unlikely that it will disappear completely through drug therapy alone. Reference to the full study on this can be found in the Contacts and Resources section if you would like to find out more.

Of course, there are advancements daily in behavioural drug therapy, but I hope you will not have to resort to this and that the advice I have given in the book will help your dog cope better with life, and to be happier and healthier in both mind and body.

The right help is at hand
Living alongside a dog with any challenging behaviour can be immensely distressing and frustrating, especially if you feel isolated and overwhelmed. In this day of social media it is so easy to ask for advice on dog owner groups, but there is no substitute for professional help. Seek out the services of a holistic vet, experienced, certified Tellington TTouch practitioner, or qualified behaviourist (links to professional governing bodies can be found in the Contacts and Resources section).

Don't feel that just because your dog has always shown this behaviour, or because it has been going on for a long time, that he can't be helped to change. Help is at hand, you just need to start somewhere. One small change or one phone call can make a huge difference to both his life and yours.

FURTHER READING

All Wrapped up for Pets: Improving function, performance and behaviour with Tellington TTouch Body Wraps by Robyn Hood (available from TTEAM offices – see Contacts & Resources for details are as an eBook from **http://www.tteam-ttouch.ca/shop/index.php?productID=259)**

Bach Flower Remedies for Dogs by Martin J Scott and Gael Mariani *(Findhorn Press)*

Beyond the Bowl by Diane Kasperowicz & Jodie White *(Woof & Co)*

Canine Behaviour: A Photo Illustrated Handbook by Barbara Handelman *(First Stone)*

Canine Nutrigenomics: The New Science of Feeding Your Dog for Optimum Health by Dr Jean Dodds & Diana R Laverdure *(Dogwise Publishing)*

Do As I Do: Using Social Learning to Train Dogs by Claudia Fugazza *(First Stone)*

Getting in TTouch with Your Dog: A gentle approach to influencing behaviour, health and performance by Linda Tellington-Jones *(Quiller Publishing)*

Harnessing your Dog's Perfection: Helping your dog be the best they can be on leash and in life with the Tellington TTouch Method by Robyn Hood & Mandy Pretty *(available from TTEAM offices – see Contacts & Resources for contact details)*

Help Your Dog Heal Itself: A-Z guide to using essential oils and herbs for hidden and common problems through the aromatic language of dogs by Caroline Ingraham *(Ingraham Trading Ltd)*

Homeopathic Care for Cats and Dogs by Don Hamilton, DVM *(North Atlantic Books)*

No Walks, No Worries: maintaining wellbeing in dogs on restricted exercise by Sian Ryan and Helen Zulch *(Hattie & Hubble)*

On Talking Terms with Dogs by Turid Rugaas *(First Stone)*

Real Dog Yoga by Jo-Rosie Haffenden *(The Pet Book Publishing Company)*

Smellorama! Nose Games for Your Dog by Viviane Theby *(Hubble & Hattie)*

Teach My Dog to do That by Jo-Rosie Haffenden & Nando Brown *(Boxtree)*

The Best Dog Diet Ever by Caroline Griffiths *(Love, Woof and Wonder Publishing)*

The Truth about Wolves and Dogs by Toni Shelbourne *(Hubble & Hattie)*

Unlock Your Dog's Potential: How to achieve a calm and happy canine by Sarah Fisher *(David & Charles)*

CONTACTS & RESOURCES

The references provided in this chapter are for informational purposes only and do not constitute endorsement of any sources or products. Readers should be aware that the websites listed in this book may change.

ADAPTIL
Available from vets, pet shops and online.
www.adaptil.co.uk

AMERICAN HOLISTIC VETERINARY MEDICAL ASSOCIATION
www.ahvma.org

APPLIED ZOOPHARMACOGNOSY
Case studies, training, and a list of practitioners can be found at:
www.ingraham.co.uk
See also Further Reading

BACH FLOWER REMEDIES
www.bachcentre.com
www.bachfloweressences.co.uk
www.bachflowerpets.com
As well as the original Bach remedies there are other companies which produce flower remedies, and have even expanded on the original 38 remedies – for preference look for alcohol-free versions.
See also Further Reading

CANINE NUTRITION
http://www.queeniechisayscook.com/
http://thespiritualdogtrainer.com/
Or search for canine nutrition consultants

CLICKER TRAINING
www.clickertraining.com

COGNITIVE SKILLS WEBSITE
www.dognition.com

CONFIDENCE COURSE EQUIPMENT
If you would like to buy equipment specially designed for dogs, this may be a useful source:
www.activebalance-vetphysio.co.uk/

DIET
Facebook page Holistic Dog Care at **https://www.facebook.com/groups/Holisticdogcare/**
Also see Further Reading

FOOD ALLERGY SCAN
http://www.nutriscan.org/

HARNESSES
Mekuti:
www.mekuti.co.uk

TTouch UK
www.ttouchtteam.co.uk

TTouch Canada
www.tteam-ttouch.ca

Xtra Dog
www.xtradog.com

HERBALISM
British Association of Veterinary Herbalists
www.herbalvets.org.uk

HOMEOPATHY
British Association of Homeopathic Veterinary Surgeons
www.bahvs.com

HYPOTHYROIDISM
http://www.petplace.com/article/dogs/behavior-training/behavior-problems/assessment-of-

hypothyroidism-as-a-factor-in-dog-behavior-problems

Hypothyroid testing
http://www.hemopet.org/hemolife-diagnostics/veterinary-thyroid-testing.html

LONGLINE
Heim Biothane available from many shops and online retailers

PET BEHAVIOUR COUNSELLORS
Association of Pet Behaviour Counsellors
www.apbc.org.uk

PET REMEDY
www.petremedy.co.uk

REAL DOG YOGA
Info and instructor list
www.therealdogyoga.co.uk

TELLINGTON TTOUCH TRAINING
For further information about Tellington TTouch, equipment, books, DVDs and links to online videos or to contact a Tellington TTouch practitioner visit the following TTouch websites. *See also Further Reading.*

TTouch in Australia
www.listeningtowhispers.com

TTouch in Austria
www.tteam.at

Tellington TTouch Canada
5435 Rochdell Road
Vernon, B.C. V1B 3E8
www.tteam-ttouch.ca

TTouch in Germany
www.tteam.de

TTouch in Ireland
www.ttouchteam-ireland.com

TTouch in Italy
www.tteam.it

TTouch in Japan
www.ttouch.jp

TTouch in Netherlands
www.tteam-ttouch.nl

TTouch in New Zealand
www.listeningtowhispers.com

Tellington TTouch South Africa
www.ttouchsa.co.za

TTouch in Switzerland
www.tellingtonttouch.ch

Tellington TTouch UK
Tilley Farm
Bath BA2 0AB
Tel: 01761 471182
www.ttouchtteam.co.uk

Tellington TTouch USA
1713 State Road 502
Santa Fe, NM 87506
www.ttouch.com

You can watch the Tellington TTouches, and confidence course being demonstrated online: visit You Tube and search for 'Tellington TTouch for Dogs and you will find plenty of video clips.

THUNDERSHIRTS
Available from Tellington TTouch office, also
www.thundershirt.co.uk

TOYS
Kong toys
www.kongcompany.com

Nina Ottosson activity toys and puzzles
www.nina-ottosson.com

Also try searching for brain games online to find lots of books and ideas.

TRAINING & BEHAVIOUR
Association of INTOdogs
www.intodogs.org

Association of Pet Behaviour Councillors
www.apbc.com

Association of Pet Dog Trainers
www.apdt.co.uk

Association of Pet Dog Trainers (US)
www.apdt.com

TREATS
Lily's Kitchen Organic Bedtime Biscuits
www.lilyskitchen.co.uk

Pooch & Mutt Calm and Relaxed Dog Treats
www.poochandmutt.com

NOTES
Research papers references

Characteristics of compulsive tail chasing and associated risk factors in Bull Terriers: Alice A. Moon-Fanelli, phd; Nicholas H. Dodman, bvms; Thomas R. Famula, phd; Nicole Cottam, ms.

Gastrointestinal disorders in dogs with excessive licking of surfaces: VéroniqueBécuwe-Bonnet, Marie-Claude Bélanger, Diane Frank, Joane Parent, Pierre Hélie.

Randomized, controlled clinical trial of the efficacy of fluoxetine for treatment of compulsive disorders in dogs:
Mami Irimajiri, BVSc, PhD; Andrew U. Luescher, DVM, PhD, DACVB; Genefer Douglass, MS; Carol Robertson-Plouch, DVM;
Alan Zimmermann, PhD; Rebecca Hozak, PhD.

Brain structural abnormalities in Dobermann Pinschers with canine compulsive disorder:
Niwako Ogata, Timothy E. Gillis, Xiaoxu Liu, Suzanne M. Cunningham, Steven B. Lowen, Bonnie L. Adams, James Sutherland-Smith, Dionyssios Mintzopoulos, Nicholas H. Dodman, Marc J. Kaufman.

Blanket and flank sucking in Dobermann Pinschers: Journal of the American Veterinary Medical Association. 231. 907-12. 10.2460/javma.231.6.907. Moon-Fanelli, Alice & Dodman, Nicholas & Cottam, Nicole. (2007).

Genomic risk for severe canine compulsive disorder, a dog model of human OCD: 14. 1-18.Dodman, Nicholas & Ginns, E.I. & Shuster, Louis & Moon-Fanelli, A.A. & Galdzicka, Marzena & Zheng, J &

Ruhe, A.L. & Neff, M.W.. (2016).

Clinical Features and outcomes in dogs and cats with obsessive-compulsive disorder 126 case studies (1989 – 2000): Karen L. Overall and Arthur D. Dunham.

Canine Compulsive Behavior: An Overview and Phenotypic Description of Tail Chasing in Bull Terriers: Moon-Fanelli, Alice. (2017).

Measuring attention deficit and activity in dogs: A new application and validation of a human ADHD questionnaire: Judit Vas, Jozsef Topal, Eva Pech, Adam Miklosi.

Candidate genes and functional noncoding variants identified in a canine model of obsessive-compulsive disorder: Ruqi Tang, Hyun Ji Noh, Dongqing Wang, Snaevar Sigurdsson, Ross Swofford, Michele Perloski, Margaret Duxbury, Edward E Patterson, Julie Albright, Marta Castelhano, Adam Auton, Adam R Boyko, Guoping Feng, Kerstin Lindblad-Toh and Elinor K Karlsson

ABOUT THE AUTHOR

Toni Shelbourne
Canine Behaviour Practitioner, Tellington TTouch Practitioner,
Real Dog Yoga Instructor & Author.

Born into a family mad about animals, it seemed only natural that Toni would be destined for a career with them; she says 'animals just walked into our lives, sometimes arriving injured, others just flying in the window'.

She has worked with dogs and wild canids since the late 1980's; during a long and successful career with the Guide Dogs for the Blind Association she quickly progressed from kennel staff to supervisor and then to staff training. In 1997 she studied under Linda Tellington-Jones and other top Tellington TTouch Instructors, becoming one of the first pupils to qualify as a Companion Animal Practitioner in the UK. In 2000 she left GDBA to pursue her passion for the Tellington TTouch Method and is now one of the highest qualified practitioners in the UK, working with all animals including dogs, cats, small animals, birds, reptiles, wild life and non-domesticated animals.

In 2001, Toni joined the UK Wolf Conservation Trust, where she went on to become a Senior Wolf Handler and Education Officer for the organisation. Through observing the wolves at close quarters, Toni developed a unique insight into their behaviour which led her to question the prevailing popular ideas about the alpha theory in dogs – ideas which often came into direct conflict with her own knowledge and observations gained at first-hand.

In addition to her background in animal welfare and conservation issues, Toni edited the UK Wolf Conservation Trust's international magazine *Wolf Print* for two years, has contributed numerous features to national dog magazines, rescue society newsletters and website blogs and made many appearances on TV and radio. Her first book, *The Truth about Wolves & Dogs*, was published in 2012, and her second, *Among the Wolves: Memoirs of a Wolf Handler,* in 2015. Toni is co-author of the HELP! series, with many more books planned.

In 2015 Toni studied with Jo-Rosie Haffenden to become a Real Dog Yoga Instructor. This learning method was featured on *Rescue Dog to Super Dog* and fits perfectly with TTouch. In 2017 Toni updated her skills in behaviour with a qualification from the International School of Canine Psychology & Behaviour with whom she is also an affiliate.

As well as working privately with clients, Toni runs workshops, seminars, gives talks, webinars and demos in Tellington TTouch and Real Dog Yoga.

Email:
ttouch1@btconnect.com

Website:
www.tonishelbourne.co.uk

Facebook:
The Truth about Wolves & Dogs

Twitter:
@tonishelbourne

Find out more about other Help! Books on Facebook at
Canine books by Toni Shelbourne and Karen Bush

And on our website at
http://tonishelbourneandkarenbush.jimdo.com/

INDEX

Applied Zoopharmacognosy 34, 126-8
Autistim 20, 21-22
Bach Flowers 120-124
Barking 8, 12, 32, 33, 39, 95
Boredom 12, 22, 28-9, 34
Chewing 12, 34-5
Chews 60-2
Circling 8, 32
Crate 36, 45-8
Conflict 22, 30, 36
Dementia 9, 19
Diet 16, 27-8, 132-3
Digging 12, 33-4, 59-60
Drugs 133-4
Emotional 30, 35, 60, 79-60, 101, 104, 120-1
Enrichment 50-77
Exercise 18, 22, 27, 38, 50-56
Flank sucking 8, 9-12, 48
Fly snapping 8, 9, 10, 11, 32-3, 95, 133
Focal Seizures 10, 14-15, 131
Genes 10, 12, 21
Hallucinations 9, 11, 12
Health 13, 14-20, 27, 49, 80, 132

Herbal remedies 130-32
Homeopathy 124-6
Hypothyroidism 15-16
Licking 8, 16, 35-6, 48, 132
Long line 32, 37-9
Mental stimulation 50-77
Muzzle 42-5
Obsession 5, 12, 34-5, 41
Pacing 8, 12, 32-3
Pain 13, 17-19, 89
Pica 8, 12, 35-6, 42, 49, 62
Polydipsia 9, 17, 35
Polyphagia 9, 35
Psychomotor 14-15
Real Dog Yoga 62-74
Shadow chasing 7, 11, 12, 32, 95
Stress 9, 12, 14, 20, 22, 24, 34, 79
Stroking the leash 39-40
Tail chasing 8, 10, 15, 32, 82
Tellington TTouch 79-113, 115-19
Training 54-6, 74-7
Veterinary collar 47-8, 80, 132

Made in the USA
Columbia, SC
16 March 2019